What People Are Saying about *Threshold Bible Study*

D1570232

"Falling in love with the sacred Scriptures enables us to fall in deeper love with our loving God. *Threshold Bible Study* helps us see the word of God alive in us and among us."
■ **ARCHBISHOP GREGORY M. AYMOND**, *Archbishop of New Orleans*

"I find *Threshold Bible Study* to be a very compelling approach to the study of Scripture with the worthy goal of facilitating genuine, integral spiritual growth. I would highly recommend the series to pastors as a suitable tool for the spiritual growth of the faithful. May *Threshold Bible Study* grow in impact on behalf of the church and become a source of genuine benefit for all who make use of it for their spiritual growth."
■ **BISHOP ROBERT M. COERVER**, *Bishop of Lubbock*

"The church has called Scripture a 'font' and 'wellspring' for the spiritual life. *Threshold Bible Study* is one of the best sources for tapping into the biblical font. *Threshold Bible Study* offers you an encounter with the word that will make your heart come alive."
■ **TIM GRAY**, *President of the Augustine Institute, Denver*

"*Threshold Bible Study* offers solid scholarship and spiritual depth. It can be counted on for lively individual study and prayer, even while it offers spiritual riches to deepen communal conversation and reflection among the people of God."
■ **SCOTT HAHN**, *Founder and President of the St. Paul Center for Biblical Theology*

"Stephen J. Binz has a unique talent for helping ordinary folks engage the Bible with deep understanding. Graduates of our Catholic Biblical School are using his *Threshold Bible Study* to bring Scripture more fully into the lives of God's people."
■ **BJ DALY HORELL**, *Director of the Catholic Biblical School, Archdiocese of Hartford*

"Stephen Binz offers an invaluable guide that can make reading the Bible enjoyable and truly nourishing. A real education on how to read the Bible, this series prepares people to discuss Scripture and to share it in community."
■ **JACQUES NIEUVIARTS, AA**, *Professor, Institut Catholique de Toulouse, France*

"I am impressed by the way *Threshold Bible Study* opens the doors of the sacred page in an intelligent, engaging way that fosters a deeper, more meditative interaction with the word of God. Stephen Binz has carefully crafted this series for either one's daily meditation or a weekly group study with equally positive benefit. I am happy to endorse this series as a means to grow in one's friendship with Christ through the prayerful study of sacred Scripture."

ARCHBISHOP JOSEPH F. NAUMANN, *Archbishop of Kansas City in Kansas*

"I most strongly recommend this series, exceptional for its scholarly solidity, pastoral practicality, and clarity of presentation. The church owes Binz a great debt of gratitude for his generous and competent labor in the service of the word of God."

PETER C. PHAN, *Professor of Catholic Social Thought, Georgetown University*

"*Threshold Bible Study* is an enriching and enlightening approach to understanding the rich faith which the Scriptures hold for us today. Written in a clear and concise style, *Threshold Bible Study* presents solid contemporary biblical scholarship, offers questions for reflection and/or discussion, and then demonstrates a way to pray from the Scriptures. All these elements work together to offer the reader a wonderful insight into how the sacred texts of our faith can touch our lives in a profound and practical way today. I heartily recommend this series to both individuals and to Bible study groups."

ABBOT GREGORY J. POLAN, OSB, *Conception Abbey, Abbot Primate of the Benedictine Order*

"Stephen J. Binz is a consistently outstanding Catholic educator and communicator whose books on the study and application of Scripture have thoroughly enriched my Christian understanding. In our fast-moving, often confusing times, his ability to help us examine and comprehend the truth through all the noise is especially needed and valuable."

ELIZABETH SCALIA, *writer and speaker, blogger as The Anchoress*

"*Threshold Bible Study* helpfully introduces the lay reader into the life-enhancing process of *lectio divina*, individually or in a group. This series leads the reader from Bible study to personal prayer, community involvement, and active Christian commitment in the world."

SANDRA M. SCHNEIDERS, *Professor Emerita, Jesuit School of Theology, Santa Clara University*

"Stephen Binz has created an essential resource for the new evangelization rooted in the discipleship process that helps participants to unpack the treasures of the Scriptures in an engaging and accessible manner. *Threshold Bible Study* connects faith learning to faithful living, leading one to a deeper relationship with Christ and his body, the Church."

JULIANNE STANZ, *Director of New Evangelization, Diocese of Green Bay*

THRESHOLD
BIBLE STUDY

FORGIVENESS

Stephen J. Binz

TWENTY-THIRD
PUBLICATIONS
twentythirdpublications.com

TWENTY-THIRD PUBLICATIONS
One Montauk Avenue, Suite 200
New London, CT 06320
(860) 437-3012 or (800) 321-0411
www.twentythirdpublications.com

ISBN: 978-1-62785-460-3
Library of Congress Control Number: 2019938500
Printed in the U.S.A.

A division of Bayard, Inc.

Contents

LESSONS 13–18

LESSONS 19–24

LESSONS 25–30

How to Use
Threshold Bible Study

Each book in the *Threshold Bible Study* series is designed to lead you through a new doorway of biblical awareness, to accompany you across a unique threshold of understanding. The characters, places, and images that you encounter in each of these topical studies will help you explore fresh dimensions of your faith and discover richer insights for your spiritual life.

Threshold Bible Study covers biblical themes in depth in a short amount of time. Unlike more traditional Bible studies that treat a biblical book or series of books, *Threshold Bible Study* aims to address specific topics within the entire Bible. The goal is not for you to comprehend everything about each passage, but rather for you to understand what a variety of passages from different books of the Bible reveals about the topic of each study.

Threshold Bible Study offers you an opportunity to explore the entire Bible from the viewpoint of a variety of different themes. The commentary that follows each biblical passage launches your reflection about that passage and helps you begin to see its significance within the context of your contemporary experience. The questions following the commentary challenge you to understand the passage more fully and apply it to your own life. The prayer starter helps conclude your study by integrating learning into your relationship with God.

These studies are designed for maximum flexibility. Each study is presented in a workbook format, with sections for reading, reflecting, writing, discussing, and praying. Space for writing after each question is ideal for personal study and allows group members to prepare in advance for their discussion. The thirty lessons in each topic may be used by an individual over the period of a month, or by a group for six sessions, with lessons to be studied each week before the next group meeting. These studies are ideal for Bible study groups, small Christian communities, adult faith formation, student groups, Sunday school, neighborhood groups, and family reading, as well as for individual learning.

The method of *Threshold Bible Study* is rooted in the classical tradition of *lectio divina*, an ancient yet contemporary means for reading the Scriptures reflectively and prayerfully. Reading and interpreting the text (*lectio*) is followed by reflective meditation on its message (*meditatio*). This reading and reflecting flows into prayer from the heart (*oratio* and *contemplatio*).

This ancient method assures us that Bible study is a matter of both the mind and the heart. It is not just an intellectual exercise to learn more and be able to discuss the Bible with others. It is, more importantly, a transforming experience. Reflecting on God's word, guided by the Holy Spirit, illumines the mind with wisdom and stirs the heart with zeal.

Following the personal Bible study, *Threshold Bible Study* offers a method for extending personal *lectio divina* into a weekly conversation with a small group. This communal experience will allow participants to enhance their appreciation of the message and build up a spiritual community (*collatio*). The end result will be to increase not only individual faith, but also faithful witness in the context of daily life (*operatio*).

Through the spiritual disciplines of Scripture reading, study, reflection, conversation, and prayer, you will experience God's grace more abundantly as your life is rooted more deeply in Christ. The risen Jesus said: "Listen! I am standing at the door, knocking; if you hear my voice and open the door, I will come in to you and eat with you, and you with me" (Rev 3:20). Listen to the word of God, open the door, and cross the threshold to an unimaginable dwelling with God!

SUGGESTIONS FOR INDIVIDUAL STUDY

- Make your Bible reading a time of prayer. Ask for God's guidance as you read the Scriptures.

- Try to study daily, or as often as possible according to the circumstances of your life.

- Read the Bible passage carefully, trying to understand both its meaning and its personal application as you read. Some persons find it helpful to read the passage aloud.

- Read the passage in another Bible translation. Each version adds to your understanding of the original text.

- Allow the commentary to help you comprehend and apply the scriptural text. The commentary is only a beginning, not the last word, on the meaning of the passage.

- After reflecting on each question, write out your responses. The very act of writing will help you clarify your thoughts, bring new insights, and amplify your understanding.

- As you reflect on your answers, think about how you can live God's word in the context of your daily life.

- Conclude each daily lesson by reading the prayer and continuing with your own prayer from the heart.

- Make sure your reflections and prayers are matters of both the mind and the heart. A true encounter with God's word is always a transforming experience.

- Choose a word or a phrase from the lesson to carry with you throughout the day as a reminder of your encounter with God's life-changing word.

- Share your learning experience with at least one other person whom you trust for additional insights and affirmation. The ideal way to share learning is in a small group that meets regularly.

SUGGESTIONS FOR GROUP STUDY

- Meet regularly; weekly is ideal. Try to be on time and make attendance a high priority for the sake of the group. The average group meets for about an hour.

- Open each session with a prepared prayer, a song, or a reflection. Find some appropriate way to bring the group from the workaday world into a sacred time of graced sharing.

- If you have not been together before, name tags are very helpful as a group begins to become acquainted with the other group members.

- Spend the first session getting acquainted with one another, reading the Introduction aloud, and discussing the questions that follow.

- Appoint a group facilitator to provide guidance to the discussion. The role of facilitator may rotate among members each week. The facilitator simply keeps the discussion on track; each person shares responsibility for the group. There is no need for the facilitator to be a trained teacher.

- Try to study the six lessons on your own during the week. When you have done your own reflection and written your own answers, you will be better prepared to discuss the six scriptural lessons with the group. If you have not had an opportunity to study the passages during the week, meet with the group anyway to share support and insights.

- Participate in the discussion as much as you are able, offering your thoughts, insights, feelings, and decisions. You learn by sharing with others the fruits of your study.

- Be careful not to dominate the discussion. It is important that everyone in the group be offered an equal opportunity to share the results of their work. Try to link what you say to the comments of others so that the group remains on the topic.

- When discussing your own personal thoughts or feelings, use "I" language. Be as personal and honest as appropriate and be very cautious about giving advice to others.

- Listen attentively to the other members of the group so as to learn from their insights. The words of the Bible affect each person in a different way, so a group provides a wealth of understanding for each member.

- Don't fear silence. Silence in a group is as important as silence in personal study. It allows individuals time to listen to the voice of God's Spirit and the opportunity to form their thoughts before they speak.

- Solicit several responses for each question. The thoughts of different people will build on the answers of others and will lead to deeper insights for all.

- Don't fear controversy. Differences of opinions are a sign of a healthy and honest group. If you cannot resolve an issue, continue on, agreeing to disagree. There is probably some truth in each viewpoint.

- Discuss the questions that seem most important for the group. There is no need to cover all the questions in the group session.

- Realize that some questions about the Bible cannot be resolved, even by experts. Don't get stuck on some issue for which there are no clear answers.

- Whatever is said in the group is said in confidence and should be regarded as such.

- Pray as a group in whatever way feels comfortable. Pray for the members of your group throughout the week.

Schedule for Group Study

Session 1: Introduction   Date: _____

Session 2: Lessons 1–6   Date: _____

Session 3: Lessons 7–12   Date: _____

Session 4: Lessons 13–18   Date: _____

Session 5: Lessons 19–24   Date: _____

Session 6: Lessons 25–30   Date: _____

MATTHEW 18:9

... times no listen to them, tell it to the church; and if the offender refuses to listen even to the church, let such a one be to you as a Gentile and a tax collector. [18] Truly I tell you, whatever you bind on earth will be bound in heaven, and whatever you loose on earth will be loosed in heaven. [19] Again, truly I tell you, if two of you agree on earth about anything you ask, it will be done for you by my Father in heaven. [20] For where two or three are gathered in my name, I am there among them."

21 Then Peter came and said to him, "Lord, if another member of the church* sins against me, how often should I forgive? As many as seven times?" [22] Jesus said to him, "Not seven times, but, I tell you, seventy-seven[1] times.

**Forgive your neighbor the wrong he has done,
and then your sins will be pardoned when you pray.**
SIRACH 28:2

Forgiveness

There is nothing natural, instinctual, or easy about forgiveness. It can be one of life's most difficult challenges. Yet we know from Scripture, psychological research, and human experience that refusing to forgive does no one any good. It can bind us in depression, anxiety, and low self-esteem. That's why studies, articles, books, and courses on forgiveness are plentiful. Practicing forgiveness is good for our physical, mental, emotional, and spiritual health. That's why Jesus said we must forgive over and over those who hurt us—seventy-seven times, to be exact. And throughout his life, he showed us the way to forgive.

If forgiveness is such a good thing, then why is it so hard? The reasons are many. When we have been emotionally wounded by another—a spouse, parent, trusted friend, a person with authority or responsibility over us—our instinctual response is usually anger and resentment, which are addictive. As our injuries fester, we may be filled with thoughts of retribution or revenge. Or we learn to self-identify as a victim, a character trait that is difficult to overcome. Our moods may become increasingly bitter, and new relationships may become hard to form. Our inability to resolve our situation makes us feel trapped in our negative emotions, leading at times to self-destructive behavior.

Because our wounds go deep, forgiveness often requires a difficult process of grieving and healing, a route that looks and feels different for everyone.

1

The core of that process is forgiveness itself, the letting go of a grievance or judgment held against someone else. When we forgive, we also let go of feelings of resentment, bitterness, and vengeance, allowing ourselves to heal and work toward wholeness. But while this may sound good in theory, in practice forgiveness can sometimes feel impossible.

Because we are human and live in a sinful world, every person gets hurt—some more than others, some worse than others. And after the wrong and the initial wave of emotions have passed, we are all presented with the question of whether and how to forgive the offender and let go of the pain, the emotional misery, the prison that is holding us back from all the potential of the future. Those who choose forgiveness will gradually move beyond the pain and open themselves to hope again; those who choose not to forgive might dwell in the bitter feelings for the rest of their lives.

Reflection and discussion

- What are some of the best reasons to practice forgiveness?

- Why do people sometimes find it impossible to forgive?

Understanding the Dynamics of Forgiveness

We are fearful and hesitant about forgiveness because we don't understand it. We think that by forgiving we are letting the other person get away with wrongdoing or opening ourselves up to be hurt again. We think that forgiveness means forgetting the offense or pretending that nothing significant happened. But genuine forgiveness implies none of these.

Before we can come to understand forgiveness, we must know what it is not:

Forgiveness does not deny the wrong or the injustice done. In fact, before forgiveness can be effective, we must acknowledge that we have indeed been wronged and that we have a right to be angry, to grieve our losses, and to feel our emotional pain. We are certainly not excusing the wrongs done to us. Rather, we are finding ways to engage deeply with our history, learn through the hurt, and begin again with greater wisdom.

Forgiveness does not mean forgetting. We can't help but remember painful experiences. Remembering helps us avoid similar experiences in the future. We must not brush aside wrongs done to us as if they never happened. The process of forgiveness does not produce amnesia, but it enables us to remember without being emotionally bound by the past. We're not saying that everything is now okay and that we have no more feelings about the harm; we are saying that we have discovered a way past the wrong and its pain.

Forgiveness is not just acceptance of a past reality. Some claim that forgiveness is merely a therapeutic technique for ridding oneself of painful memories and feelings. But genuine forgiveness involves a relationship between persons. The wrong occurred in an interpersonal context: one person wrongs another. Hence, forgiveness is directed toward the person who offended; it is a voluntary gift of mercy from the one who has been offended.

Forgiveness is not a moment but a process. Forgiveness takes time, and we should not attempt it until we feel we are ready. There is no prescribed time frame, no generalized benchmark for the forgiveness process. It takes as long as it takes. But through the process, we learn more about ourselves, our boundaries, and our needs. We change and become more emotionally and spiritually mature.

Forgiveness does not necessarily lead to reconciliation. We mistakenly imagine forgiveness involves saying "I forgive you" to our offender, followed by a hug or a gesture that all is absolved. This may happen sometimes, but it is not the norm. Forgiving another does not mean that we have to continue including the other person in our life. Relationships that involve continuing abuse must be abandoned. And forgiving another does not imply that we necessarily have to communicate our forgiveness to the other. We can forgive people we should best not see again and even those who have died. Forgiveness does not mean reconciling the relationship. A restored relationship, for those who choose it, is a further process beyond forgiveness.

Forgiveness is an intentional and voluntary process. We cannot be forced to forgive another or be shamed into it. It isn't something we do for the person who wronged us. Our initial motivation for beginning the process of forgiveness is to stop our own pain. We want to be able to heal and move on. We are the first beneficiaries of the change in attitude and perspective we experience when we decide to forgive. The release of toxic anger and bitter resentment we experience makes us feel better. These changes then have their effect on all our other relationships and activities.

The emphasis on forgiveness throughout Scripture is due to the fact that it is good for us. We are healthier and happier when we forgive. Because forgiveness doesn't come easily or innately, God's word instructs us on how to practice it. Texts throughout the Bible underscore God's forgiveness of his people, showing us that when we forgive others, we are imitating God, living in the divine image. Our offender may not deserve our forgiveness, just as we may not deserve God's forgiveness. We may not want to forgive, but God requires it of us and offers us the grace to accomplish it.

Deciding to forgive is the first step on a mysterious, divine journey. The way is not a straight line; usually it feels more like a spiral, experiencing over and over again feelings of anger, relief, confusion, comfort, anxiety, and release. Like the way of the exodus, when God made the Israelites his own people, the journey feels painful, but it brings freedom. As time goes by, unbearable memories dissipate and a life of peace and wholeness comes into view.

Although we know we can't change the past, we can change our attitudes toward past injustices and suffering by integrating them into the larger context of our lives. Did the experience make me stronger, more empathic of others, more courageous? Did others somehow gain through what I endured and how I matured? When we're angry, bitter, and self-absorbed, we cannot be creative and open to new experiences, but finding meaning in the painful experiences of the past leads us to deeper acceptance. Scripture helps us find this meaning and purpose in the forgiveness process.

As forgivers we must gradually give up resentment and replace it with compassion, the recognition that we all suffer together. Compassionate people are able to discover the faults and flaws of others within themselves. The sins we see so easily in others are our sins too. As compassionate people, we understand that everyone shares this suffering world together.

At some point in the process of forgiveness, we must move from a focus on ourselves to a focus on the offenders, coming to realize that they are flawed because all human beings are flawed, that they speak and act from distorted ideas and understandings, and that they struggle like the rest of humanity. Eventually, we must decide to give to the offenders the gift of forgiveness, even though they don't deserve it. Then, paradoxically, we begin to heal in the process of offering this compassion. Through the process of forgiveness, we give up our right to seething anger and hostility, replacing them with mercy toward the wrongdoers, and relationships are changed through human compassion and divine grace.

A clear sign that forgiveness is taking its course is our lack of resentful feelings, negative thoughts, and harmful behaviors toward the offenders and their replacement with goodwill and kindness. Jesus taught us to live in love, whether it be toward our neighbors or toward our enemies. Forgiveness is an act of love toward God, our offenders, and ourselves. Loving others, while protecting ourselves from harm, is a sign of the transformed life we receive through faith in him.

Reflection and discussion

- How is my misunderstanding of forgiveness being corrected?

- What new insights about forgiveness am I gaining?

Forgiveness in, with, and through the Word of God

The source of the Christian understanding of forgiveness is the revelation of God, who is willing to bear the cost of forgiveness in order to redeem humanity and bring us to the fullness of life. In response to this divine forgiveness, God calls us to embody forgiveness through practices like repentance, confessing our sins, showing compassion, repairing brokenness, and forgiving others. So, forgiveness is not just a word spoken, a feeling felt, or an isolated action performed, but a tangible practice and way of life in imitation of God.

The centrality of forgiveness in divine revelation and Christian practice prevents us from thinking about forgiveness as merely a private transaction between God and an individual or between two persons. We forgive, not in isolation, but only with the grace of God in the context of community. We become more forgiving of others when we simultaneously learn to experience what it means to be forgiven—by God and by others.

As people baptized into Christ, we learn that forgiveness requires a dying and rising—dying to our old selves bound to past sin, and being raised in newness of life. God's forgiving grace gives us a new perspective on our histories of betrayal and being betrayed. Living as the body of Christ in the world, we practice forgiveness by unlearning patterns of sin and struggling for healing wherever there is brokenness. By forgiving and being forgiven, we become a sign of God's kingdom, the kingdom that Jesus announced and enacted, by offering new life in the face of evil and sin.

The call to Christian discipleship always implies a call to share in the work of forgiveness and to bear the Christlike suffering involved in that work. As disciples of Jesus, we realize that forgiveness is not simply a release from the past but a commitment to the future. Costly forgiveness requires that we transform the patterns of our relationships with God and with one another. Living a cruciform life means that we do not possess our lives; we give them over to Christ, and in doing so our lives are transformed as we share in his divine life.

Discerning precisely how we ought to practice forgiveness in specific social circumstances and individual situations involves the work of the Holy Spirit. We learn how to practice this discernment well through holy exemplars, especially the saints, whose lives testify to the difficult and often heroic work of forgiveness. Costly forgiveness requires such practices as confronting sin, love of enemies, and works of mercy.

God's forgiveness is both the first and final word of the Christian life. In this time between Christ's first and final coming, we must prepare the way for God's ultimate judgment and forgiveness. Experiencing God's forgiveness now sets us on mission to the larger world. Preparing the way for the Lord's coming entails specific practices that enable people to hear and receive the ultimate message of God's forgiveness and healing grace. Studying Scripture, receiving the sacraments, practicing contemplative prayer, engaging in Christian witness, and living the communal life—all prepare the way for the full realization of God's kingdom.

Commitment to the future means helping to create a culture of forgiveness on a community level and in our society. Many refuse to embody God's forgiveness and remain trapped in histories and habits of evil and sin. We know that vengeful anger over injustices can transfer to entire groups of people and can be transmitted from one generation to another. Revenge creates more victims, and the angry victims then demand revenge. Social movements are emerging throughout the world in which forgiveness is a central component of helping people heal from hatred, violence, and war. Education in forgiveness and experiments in personal practices of forgiveness equip people to respond with mercy and break the cycles of retaliation and victimization. People who are taught how to forgive learn how to overcome anger and hurt, become more optimistic and self-confident, and begin to practice compassion and forgiveness in a variety of situations.

Truthfulness in communities and societies is only possible where wrong has been uncovered and forgiven. And when people experience a state of truthfulness through acknowledgment of their own wrongs, they are not afraid or ashamed to tell the truth wherever it must be told. Forgiveness is possible even under the most brutal and unfair circumstances. The revelation of our God teaches us that no act, no matter how terrible, is unforgivable. Holiness requires prophetic action directed at situations where people's lives are being diminished and destroyed, and forgiveness is an essential dimension of the necessary healing for life to flourish again.

Reflection and discussion

- What is the meaning of the phrase, "To err is human, to forgive divine," by the poet Alexander Pope?

- Why is forgiveness necessary on both an individual and societal level?

Experiencing Scripture's Transforming Power

Genesis ends with the beautiful scene of Joseph forgiving his brothers for their terrible wrongs against him. This scene of forgiveness leads into all the other books of the Bible, because it allows for the preservation of the sons of Jacob and God's rescue of their descendants from the slavery of Egypt. In Israel's Torah, God is shown to be a personal God, rich in mercy and forgiveness, as Moses pleads for the people during their journey through the wilderness. King David, too, learns how to admit his sin and turn to God for forgiveness, teaching his son Solomon how to intercede on behalf of God's people in their sin. Although God's forgiveness does not remove the consequences of Israel's sins, it does enable them to begin again and look to the future whenever they turn to God with repentance.

The psalms teach God's people how to speak the truth about their wrongs, turn back to God, and open their lives in confidence to God's forgiveness. The prophets plead for God's forgiveness, teaching the Israelites to await the complete forgiveness that God promises in the new covenant. As we read the word of God spoken through the ancient Torah, prophets, and psalms, we realize that God is speaking to us, the spiritual descendants of the Israelites. God always longs to confer forgiveness on his people, and our ancestors in the Old Testament teach us how to release our hearts to receive it.

The gospels demonstrate that God's forgiveness is proclaimed and enacted through the life, death, and resurrection of Jesus Christ. Jesus welcomes sinners and eats with them, persistently breaking barriers and showing that forgiveness is available for all. He teaches forgiveness in his parables and warns that those who do not forgive others are unable to experience God's forgiveness. He asks forgiveness for those who crucify him even though they are ignorant of what they are doing. The gospels help us recognize that sin is a reality that pervades our lives and relationships. We are not only those on whom hurts are inflicted; we are also people capable of horrible evil, including the violence that nailed Jesus to the cross.

After the resurrection, Jesus sends his disciples into the world to proclaim the good news of repentance for the forgiveness of sins. The New Testament, then, underlines the many ways that Christian communities embody this forgiveness as they live out their mission. The focus of forgiveness shifts from the temple and its sacrifices to the church and its ministers who are authorized by Jesus to forgive in his name. This global community of forgiven and forgiving people becomes the living sign of God's kingdom, fulfilling the purpose and destiny of humanity through its loving communion with God and with one another.

The Scriptures demonstrate that Christ's forgiveness takes different forms in every circumstance. Although the Lord's death is the definitive sacrifice for the sin of the world, the Holy Spirit guides us as we reflect on the Scriptures and discern how to embody Christ's forgiveness in specific practices in many diverse circumstances. The Spirit, who gives the Scriptures their transforming power, works powerfully within us as we reflect on the sacred texts and open our lives more fully to God's living word. Let us implore the Spirit to work deeply in our hearts so that we may become instruments of divine forgiveness in the world.

Reflection and discussion

- How might God's word in Scripture broaden my understanding of forgiveness?

- In what way do I desire God to transform my life through this study of God's word?

Prayer

Creator and Redeemer of your people, who sent your Son to embody the forgiveness you desire for all people, send your Holy Spirit to guide, encourage, and enlighten me as I begin this study of your inspired Scriptures. Let these sacred texts so transform my mind and heart that I may reflect your image in the world and become an instrument of your forgiveness. Make me compassionate so that I may suffer with others by recognizing the sins I see in others within my own heart. Give me hope for a renewed world, and help me devote my energies to the difficult work of creating a culture of forgiveness and a civilization of love.

SUGGESTIONS FOR FACILITATORS, GROUP SESSION 1

1. If the group is meeting for the first time, or if there are newcomers joining the group, it is helpful to provide name tags.

2. Distribute the books to the members of the group.

3. You may want to ask the participants to introduce themselves and tell the group a bit about themselves.

4. Ask one or more of these introductory questions:
   - What drew you to join this group?
   - What is your biggest fear in beginning this Bible study?
   - How is beginning this study like a "threshold" for you?

5. You may want to pray this prayer as a group:
   Come upon us, Holy Spirit, to enlighten and guide us as we begin this study of forgiveness. You inspired the biblical authors to express your word as manifested to the people of Israel and most fully in the life of Jesus. Motivate us each day to read the Scriptures and deepen our understanding and love for these sacred texts. Bless us during this session and throughout the coming week with the fire of your love.

6. Read the Introduction aloud, pausing at each question for discussion. Group members may wish to write the insights of the group as each question is discussed. Encourage several members of the group to respond to each question.

7. Don't feel compelled to finish the complete Introduction during the session. It is better to allow sufficient time to talk about the questions raised than to rush to the end. Group members may read any remaining sections on their own after the group meeting.

8. Instruct group members to read the first six lessons on their own during the six days before the next group meeting. They should write out their own answers to the questions as preparation for next week's group discussion.

9. Fill in the date for each group meeting under "Schedule for Group Study."

10. Conclude by praying aloud together the prayer at the end of the Introduction.

**"Please forgive the crime of the servants of the God
of your father." Joseph wept when they spoke to him.
Then his brothers also wept.** GENESIS 50:17–18

Joseph Forgives
His Brothers

GENESIS 50:15–21 [15]*Realizing that their father was dead, Joseph's brothers said, "What if Joseph still bears a grudge against us and pays us back in full for all the wrong that we did to him?"* [16]*So they approached Joseph, saying, "Your father gave this instruction before he died,* [17]*'Say to Joseph: I beg you, forgive the crime of your brothers and the wrong they did in harming you.' Now therefore please forgive the crime of the servants of the God of your father." Joseph wept when they spoke to him.* [18]*Then his brothers also wept, fell down before him, and said, "We are here as your slaves."* [19]*But Joseph said to them, "Do not be afraid! Am I in the place of God?* [20]*Even though you intended to do harm to me, God intended it for good, in order to preserve a numerous people, as he is doing today.* [21]*So have no fear; I myself will provide for you and your little ones." In this way he reassured them, speaking kindly to them.*

Joseph was the envy of his brothers, the other eleven sons of Jacob. So, out of jealousy and spite, they sold their brother to some merchants, telling their father that Joseph had been killed by wild beasts (Gen 37). Their little brother was sold again and eventually became the ruler of Pharaoh's Egypt. So when a famine came upon the land of Canaan, Joseph's brothers

came to Egypt to obtain food. There they requested grain from Egypt's officials, and in a tearful reunion Joseph revealed himself to them (Gen 45).

Many years later, after the death and burial of their father, Joseph's brothers fear that he might still hold a grudge against them and pay them back for
their crimes against him (verse 15). They tell him that their father's dying
wish was for Joseph to forgive his brothers for all the wrong they had done
against him (verses 16–17). So they plead for Joseph to forgive them.

The brothers do not minimize the wrong they had done; they even call
their actions of many years ago a "crime." Nor does Joseph deny the wrongs
of his brothers or the pain their transgressions have caused him. But in forgiving his brothers, Joseph gives up any desire for vengeance he might have har-
bored. Joseph weeps, overcome with emotions as he remembers the misery
of being alone in the dark pit, being sold to traitors, and spending years in
Egyptian prisons. Yet he also weeps at the guilt and anxiety his brothers still
feel, as well as for the joy of being reunited with them and their expression of
remorse for their crimes.

When his brothers fall down before him weeping, Joseph addresses them,
urging them to have no fears (verse 19). Joseph allays their anxieties, convinc-
ing them that he has no interest in seeking revenge. His soul was no longer
imprisoned by the wrongs they had done him. Joseph tells them that he is not
"in the place of God," to whom alone belongs the right of punitive vindica-
tion. Moreover, he emphasizes the vast difference between human intentions
and God's way of working. Whereas his brother had planned to do him harm,
"God intended it for good" (verse 20).

Beyond human knowledge, desire, or realization, God may use our evil
purposes as the instrument for ultimate good. Throughout the whole ordeal
of Joseph, God has protected him, elevating him to leadership in Egypt at
a crucial time, enabling him to save the lives of his family and the lives of
numerous peoples throughout the region. God can handle every situation for
those who trust in him, no matter how menacing, to bring good out of human
greed, envy, and hatred.

Finally, Joseph promises that he will continue to provide for his brothers and their families (verse 20). As the famine continued, they would have
plenty of food to eat and they could shepherd their flocks in security. Joseph's
promise, as well as his reassurance and his comfort, provides concrete evi-

dence of his forgiveness. By walking through the door of forgiveness, Joseph and his brothers could enter into whatever future they would shape for themselves.

The study of Joseph and his brothers teaches us that we do not have to deny the past in order to forgive. We can confront our offenders with the reality of what they did and let them see our pain. We can forgive others for their very real offenses, then let God use our suffering for good purposes. As we are filled more and more with the wonder of God's providence, we can free ourselves from the pains of the past and look to the future with hope.

Reflection and discussion

- What in the account of Joseph and his brothers indicates that forgiveness implies neither excusing the offender nor forgetting about the offense?

- What indicates that Joseph's forgiveness of his brothers was sincere and genuine?

Prayer

God of our fathers and mothers, who called our spiritual ancestors to the task of forgiveness, work among your people today to bring the healing and joyful future that only forgiveness can provide.

"The Lord, the Lord, a God merciful and gracious,
slow to anger, and abounding in steadfast love and faithfulness,
keeping steadfast love for the thousandth generation,
forgiving iniquity and transgression and sin."

EXODUS 34:6–7

God Forgives Iniquity, Transgression, and Sin

EXODUS 32:30–34 ³⁰*On the next day Moses said to the people, "You have sinned a great sin. But now I will go up to the Lord; perhaps I can make atonement for your sin." ³¹So Moses returned to the Lord and said, "Alas, this people has sinned a great sin; they have made for themselves gods of gold. ³²But now, if you will only forgive their sin—but if not, blot me out of the book that you have written." ³³But the Lord said to Moses, "Whoever has sinned against me I will blot out of my book. ³⁴But now go, lead the people to the place about which I have spoken to you; see, my angel shall go in front of you. Nevertheless, when the day comes for punishment, I will punish them for their sin."*

EXODUS 34:1–10 ¹*The Lord said to Moses, "Cut two tablets of stone like the former ones, and I will write on the tablets the words that were on the former tablets, which you broke. ²Be ready in the morning, and come up in the morning to Mount Sinai and present yourself there to me, on the top of the mountain. ³No one shall come up with you, and do not let anyone be seen throughout all the mountain; and do not let flocks or herds graze in front of that mountain." ⁴So Moses* *cut two tablets of stone like the former ones; and he rose early in the morning and went up on Mount Sinai, as the Lord had commanded him, and took in his hand the two tablets of stone.* ⁵*The Lord descended in the cloud and stood with him there, and proclaimed the name, "The Lord."* ⁶*The Lord passed before him, and proclaimed,*

> *"The Lord, the Lord,*
> *a God merciful and gracious,*
> *slow to anger,*
> *and abounding in steadfast love and faithfulness,*
> ⁷*keeping steadfast love for the thousandth generation,*
> *forgiving iniquity and transgression and sin,*
> *yet by no means clearing the guilty,*
> *but visiting the iniquity of the parents*
> *upon the children*
> *and the children's children,*
> *to the third and the fourth generation."*

⁸*And Moses quickly bowed his head toward the earth, and worshiped.* ⁹*He said, "If now I have found favor in your sight, O Lord, I pray, let the Lord go with us. Although this is a stiff-necked people, pardon our iniquity and our sin, and take us for your inheritance."*

¹⁰*He said: I hereby make a covenant. Before all your people I will perform marvels, such as have not been performed in all the earth or in any nation; and all the people among whom you live shall see the work of the Lord; for it is an awesome thing that I will do with you.*

The heart of the Old Testament is the unique relationship that God established with the Israelites at Mount Sinai. They would be God's treasured possession if they obeyed his voice and kept the covenant. But before Moses could descend the mountain, God's people created a crisis by making a golden calf to worship. God's just anger flared, and Moses shattered the tablets of the covenant at the foot of the mountain, indicating that the relationship had been terminated.

By creating the golden calf, the Israelites have violated God's exclusive claim upon his people, as expressed in the commandments of the covenant.

They have "sinned a great sin" (verses 30–31), for which they are deserving of God's punishment. This choice of another god or of worshiping anything but God alone defines the nature of sin. They have alienated themselves from God and broken their covenant, raising the question of whether a continuing relationship between the holy God and sinful people is possible.

The intervention of Moses indicates the struggle involved with restoring a broken covenant. When all seemed to be lost, the only possible resolution is found in the character of God. Instructing Moses to create two new stone tablets, God meets Moses on the mountain to give him a new revelation, defining the divine nature as merciful, faithful, and forgiving (verses 6–7). Yet, as God insists here, forgiveness of "iniquity and transgression and sin" does not eliminate the just treatment of wrongdoing. Forgiveness is not remission of punishment, since suffering is a natural consequence of sin. Forgiveness between God and his people, rather, is the reestablishment of a broken relationship.

Wrongdoing has inevitable costs, but God's forgiveness assures his people that it need not cut off the possibility of a better future. Saying that consequences of iniquity are visited "to the third and fourth generation" acknowledges that the effects of any one person's sin brings suffering upon the whole family and tribe, affecting the lives of every living generation. In contrast, however, God's steadfast love and forgiveness remains "for the thousandth generation." While offering a realistic understanding of the effects of sin, the revelation assures us that God does not hold on to resentment but lets go of iniquity in order to give his people hope.

Moses responds to this new revelation of God's nature in the only appropriate way: he "bowed his head toward the earth, and worshiped" (verse 8). The revelation of God as compassionate and forgiving stands in contrast to the gods of other nations. God's character does not reflect human nature or echo the human personality. While confrontations between ancient peoples were frequently settled with violence, and their gods reflected their vengeful nature, Israel's God is described as compassionate and forgiving because Israel's encounters with God in history led them to insist that this is what God is like. Israel professed a God who would lead his people, in time, to imitate the divine character and to share in the divine nature.

Reflection and discussion

- In what way is all sin somehow a violation of our relationship with God?

- The psalmist sings, "You were a forgiving God to them, but an avenger of their wrongdoings" (Ps 99:8). What does this express about the nature of God's forgiveness?

- How have I experienced wrongdoing affecting "the third and fourth generation"? What experience has convinced me that God's forgiveness remains "for the thousandth generation"?

Prayer

Liberating God, who is merciful and gracious to the thousandth generation, forgive the iniquity and sins of your people. Open my heart to your transforming power so that I may be like you and reflect your divine nature in the world.

He shall slaughter the goat of the sin offering that
is for the people and bring its blood inside the curtain,
and do with its blood as he did with the blood of the bull,
sprinkling it upon the mercy seat and before the mercy seat.

LEVITICUS 16:15

A Sin Offering for God's People

LEVITICUS 16:2–22 ²*The Lord said to Moses:*

Tell your brother Aaron not to come just at any time into the sanctuary inside the curtain before the mercy seat that is upon the ark, or he will die; for I appear in the cloud upon the mercy seat. ³*Thus shall Aaron come into the holy place: with a young bull for a sin offering and a ram for a burnt offering.* ⁴*He shall put on the holy linen tunic, and shall have the linen undergarments next to his body, fasten the linen sash, and wear the linen turban; these are the holy vestments. He shall bathe his body in water, and then put them on.* ⁵*He shall take from the congregation of the people of Israel two male goats for a sin offering, and one ram for a burnt offering.*

⁶*Aaron shall offer the bull as a sin offering for himself, and shall make atonement for himself and for his house.* ⁷*He shall take the two goats and set them before the Lord at the entrance of the tent of meeting;* ⁸*and Aaron shall cast lots on the two goats, one lot for the Lord and the other lot for Azazel.* ⁹*Aaron shall present the goat on which the lot fell for the Lord, and offer it as a sin offering;* ¹⁰*but the goat on which the lot fell for Azazel shall be presented alive before the Lord to make atonement over it, that it may be sent away into the wilderness to Azazel.*

¹¹*Aaron shall present the bull as a sin offering for himself, and shall make atonement for himself and for his house; he shall slaughter the bull as a sin offering for himself.* ¹²*He shall take a censer full of coals of fire from the altar before the Lord, and two handfuls of crushed sweet incense, and he shall bring it inside the curtain* ¹³*and put the incense on the fire before the Lord, that the cloud of the incense may cover the mercy seat that is upon the covenant, or he will die.* ¹⁴*He shall take some of the blood of the bull, and sprinkle it with his finger on the front of the mercy seat, and before the mercy seat he shall sprinkle the blood with his finger seven times.*

¹⁵*He shall slaughter the goat of the sin offering that is for the people and bring its blood inside the curtain, and do with its blood as he did with the blood of the bull, sprinkling it upon the mercy seat and before the mercy seat.* ¹⁶*Thus he shall make atonement for the sanctuary, because of the uncleannesses of the people of Israel, and because of their transgressions, all their sins; and so he shall do for the tent of meeting, which remains with them in the midst of their uncleannesses* ¹⁷*No one shall be in the tent of meeting from the time he enters to make atonement in the sanctuary until he comes out and has made atonement for himself and for his house and for all the assembly of Israel.* ¹⁸*Then he shall go out to the altar that is before the Lord and make atonement on its behalf, and shall take some of the blood of the bull and of the blood of the goat, and put it on each of the horns of the altar.* ¹⁹*He shall sprinkle some of the blood on it with his finger seven times, and cleanse it and hallow it from the uncleannesses of the people of Israel.*

²⁰*When he has finished atoning for the holy place and the tent of meeting and the altar, he shall present the live goat.* ²¹*Then Aaron shall lay both his hands on the head of the live goat, and confess over it all the iniquities of the people of Israel, and all their transgressions, all their sins, putting them on the head of the goat, and sending it away into the wilderness by means of someone designated for the task.* ²²*The goat shall bear on itself all their iniquities to a barren region; and the goat shall be set free in the wilderness.*

Leviticus prescribes many types of sacrifices and rituals, each expressing a recognition of the debt people owe to God as the source of life and blessing. The rites prescribed here for Israel's Day of Atonement empower the high priest (Aaron and his successors) to cleanse both the sanctuary and the people from the sin that diminishes their witness and compromises God's presence with them.

The high priest must first prepare for the annual rituals by procuring the sacrificial animals, bathing himself in water, and dressing in linen garments. After sacrificing the bull as a sin offering for himself and collecting the blood for the rite of purification, he prepares to enter "inside the curtain before the mercy seat that is upon the ark" (verse 2). This inner sanctuary, the holy of holies of the tent of meeting, could be entered only by the high priest and only once each year. Aaron enters behind the curtain with a censer of hot coals and some incense so that the cloud obscures the ark of the covenant and the mercy seat, the gold covering of the ark where God's glory was invisibly enthroned between the two golden cherubim (verses 12–13).

The high priest then sprinkles the blood of the bull with his finger seven times on the mercy seat, making atonement for his own sins (verse 14). He then does the same with the goat, sacrificing it as a sin offering and then sprinkling its blood inside the curtained sanctuary, making atonement for all the "uncleannesses," "transgressions," and "sins" of the peoples (verses 15–16). Sin has the capacity to defile not only people but even their religious institutions, extending their reach into the inner sanctuary and to the very throne of God. The Israelites know that an all-holy God will not dwell in an unholy dwelling. When God's people are faithful to the covenant, the sanctuary radiates their commitment and sustains their witness. But when they forsake their relationship with God, the sanctuary continues to reflect their failings until it is cleansed through the sacrificial blood with the prescribed rituals.

The third major element of the Day of Atonement is the ritual with the live goat, the one selected by lot "for Azazel," a demonic power residing in the wilderness. The high priest lays his hands on the head of the goat, confessing all the "iniquities," "transgressions," and "sins" of the people (verse 21). After ritually placing the wrongs of the community on the goat, the animal is sent away into the desert, far from the people and far from God's sanctuary. In this place of no return, the sins that threaten the holiness of God's people are brought far away from the Israelites and their religious institutions.

Every type of sacrifice and ritual prescribed in Leviticus prefigures a different effect of the redeeming sacrifice of Jesus Christ. Worshiping God in a transitory sanctuary, offering imperfect sacrifices through a provisional priesthood, the people of the former covenant were waiting and hoping for an experience of God they could not yet grasp. But Christ, as the high priest, bearing the sacrifice of his own blood into the presence of God, completes and perfects the rituals of the Day of Atonement. In him we can enter the intimacy of God's presence, worshiping the living God and experiencing his merciful forgiveness.

Reflection and discussion

- Why does God require that the Israelites experience forgiveness of their sins through sacrifices and religious rituals?

- Leviticus states the significance of blood: "The life of the flesh is in the blood; and I have given it to you for making atonement for your lives on the altar; for, as life, it is the blood that makes atonement" (Lev 17:11). How does this understanding of sacrificial blood help me better understand the significance of Christ's sacrifice?

- Why is the eucharistic liturgy of the new covenant described as a cosmic Day of Atonement?

Prayer

Faithful God, in every age you have offered us ways to repair human failures in our attempts to maintain our covenant with you. Forgive my wrongs and redeem my life through the sacred blood of Christ.

"Forgive the iniquity of this people according to the greatness of your steadfast love, just as you have pardoned this people, from Egypt even until now." NUMBERS 14:19

Moses Pleads for God's Forgiveness of the Israelites

NUMBERS 14:10–23 ¹⁰*Then the glory of the Lord appeared at the tent of meeting to all the Israelites.* ¹¹*And the Lord said to Moses, "How long will this people despise me? And how long will they refuse to believe in me, in spite of all the signs that I have done among them?* ¹²*I will strike them with pestilence and disinherit them, and I will make of you a nation greater and mightier than they."*

¹³*But Moses said to the Lord, "Then the Egyptians will hear of it, for in your might you brought up this people from among them,* ¹⁴*and they will tell the inhabitants of this land. They have heard that you, O Lord, are in the midst of this people; for you, O Lord, are seen face to face, and your cloud stands over them and you go in front of them, in a pillar of cloud by day and in a pillar of fire by night.* ¹⁵*Now if you kill this people all at one time, then the nations who have heard about you will say,* ¹⁶*'It is because the Lord was not able to bring this people into the land he swore to give them that he has slaughtered them in the wilderness.'* ¹⁷*And now, therefore, let the power of the Lord be great in the way that you promised when you spoke, saying,*

¹⁸*'The Lord is slow to anger,*
and abounding in steadfast love,

> *forgiving iniquity and transgression,*
> *but by no means clearing the guilty,*
> *visiting the iniquity of the parents*
> *upon the children*
> *to the third and the fourth generation.'*

[19]*Forgive the iniquity of this people according to the greatness of your steadfast love, just as you have pardoned this people, from Egypt even until now."*

[20]*Then the Lord said, "I do forgive, just as you have asked;* [21]*nevertheless—as I live, and as all the earth shall be filled with the glory of the Lord—* [22]*none of the people who have seen my glory and the signs that I did in Egypt and in the wilderness, and yet have tested me these ten times and have not obeyed my voice,* [23]*shall see the land that I swore to give to their ancestors; none of those who despised me shall see it."*

During their long journey in the wilderness, the Israelites complain about life in the wilderness and fear their future in the promised land. They conclude that they would have been better off dying in Egypt or in the desert. So they propose to choose a new leader and return to Egypt, a rebellion that would reverse God's saving action on their behalf in the exodus.

Manifesting the divine glory at the tent of meeting, the Lord speaks to Moses, crying out in lament, "How long will this people despise me? And how long will they refuse to believe in me, in spite of all the signs that I have done among them?" (verse 11). As God threatens to reverse the exodus because of the people's refusal to trust, Moses again, as at Mount Sinai, intervenes for the people before the Lord. Reminding God of his own promises concerning his merciful forgiveness (verses 17–18), Moses asks God to "forgive the iniquity of this people," in the same way that the Lord has "pardoned this people, from Egypt even until now" (verse 19). This rebellion is one of many examples of the continual offenses of the people and the necessity of God's pardon throughout their journey.

The Lord responds directly to Moses' request: "I do forgive, just as you have asked" (verse 20). But then God immediately states the consequences of the people's sin: the generation that left Egypt will not enter the promised land. Again, we see that forgiveness is not defined as the cancellation of punishment. The consequences of wrongdoing are inevitable. Rather, forgiveness is God's decision to continue the covenant relationship with the Israelites. The rebellious people continue to live out their natural life spans, but they will die before entering the promised land. The covenant with God will continue, but it will be lived by the next generation in the land.

The Lord reminds the Israelites of their "ten" rebellions, testing God and refusing to obey his voice (verse 22). God's forgiveness is not something that the Israelites deserve; it is the result of God's gracious willingness to forgive, in spite of their perennial unfaithfulness. While the emphasis of the narrative falls on God's forgiving nature, the account continues to demonstrate how both blessing and judgment flow through the generations. God forgives the Israelites, remaining committed to them. The children of the rebellious generation will inherit God's promises and enter the land. But none of those who despised God, defying the covenant and desiring to reverse God's saving will, would see the land God promised them.

The Old Testament literature expresses how the Israelites depend on the truth of God's self-definition throughout their existence. Exodus 34:6–7 is partially quoted in a variety of Old Testament texts: in narratives, in psalms of praise, in laments, and in prayers of confession for sins. Over and over, the character of God is described as merciful, faithful, and forgiving. Although the consequences of sin remain, with costs for the community for three or four generations, God does not give up on his people. Rather, God lets go of their wrongdoing and offers them renewed hope for the future.

Reflection and discussion

- In what ways does Moses try to convince God to "forgive the iniquity of this people"?

- Why does God's forgiveness not remove the consequences of Israel's sins?

- What am I learning about God's forgiveness from the experience of the Israelites?

- How have I experienced both judgment and blessing flowing through the generations of my family or community?

Prayer

Redeeming God, who has pardoned your people from Egypt even until now, help me to trust in you as I look to the future. Forgive me for my failure to put my faith in you, and let me hope in your promises.

David said to Nathan, "I have sinned against the Lord."
Nathan said to David, "Now the Lord has put away your sin;
you shall not die." 2 SAMUEL 12:13

Nathan the Prophet Brings King David to Repentance

2 SAMUEL 12:1–15 ¹*And the Lord sent Nathan to David. He came to him, and said to him, "There were two men in a certain city, the one rich and the other poor. ²The rich man had very many flocks and herds; ³but the poor man had nothing but one little ewe lamb, which he had bought. He brought it up, and it grew up with him and with his children; it used to eat of his meager fare, and drink from his cup, and lie in his bosom, and it was like a daughter to him. ⁴Now there came a traveler to the rich man, and he was loath to take one of his own flock or herd to prepare for the wayfarer who had come to him, but he took the poor man's lamb, and prepared that for the guest who had come to him." ⁵Then David's anger was greatly kindled against the man. He said to Nathan, "As the Lord lives, the man who has done this deserves to die; ⁶he shall restore the lamb fourfold, because he did this thing, and because he had no pity."*

⁷*Nathan said to David, "You are the man! Thus says the Lord, the God of Israel: I anointed you king over Israel, and I rescued you from the hand of Saul; ⁸I gave you your master's house, and your master's wives into your bosom, and gave you the house of Israel and of Judah; and if that had been too little, I would have added as much more. ⁹Why have you despised the word of the Lord, to do*

what is evil in his sight? You have struck down Uriah the Hittite with the sword, and have taken his wife to be your wife, and have killed him with the sword of the Ammonites. [10]*Now therefore the sword shall never depart from your house, for you have despised me, and have taken the wife of Uriah the Hittite to be your wife.* [11]*Thus says the Lord: I will raise up trouble against you from within your own house; and I will take your wives before your eyes, and give them to your neighbor, and he shall lie with your wives in the sight of this very sun.* [12]*For you did it secretly; but I will do this thing before all Israel, and before the sun."* [13]*David said to Nathan, "I have sinned against the Lord." Nathan said to David, "Now the Lord has put away your sin; you shall not die.* [14]*Nevertheless, because by this deed you have utterly scorned the Lord, the child that is born to you shall die."* [15]*Then Nathan went to his house.*

David's sin with Bathsheba and its aftermath is the turning point in the narrative of the king's reign. Inattentive to his responsibilities while his soldiers are fighting a desperate battle on his behalf, David engages in self-serving behavior. Strutting on top of his palace—superior, domineering, and self-absorbed—David gazes down on his capital city and spies the beautiful Bathsheba. After her intercourse with the king, Bathsheba informs him that she is pregnant. So David, desiring to protect himself, seeks to create a cover-up, concealing his sin rather than facing it.

Calling her husband, Uriah, from the battlefield and sending him home with his wife, David seeks to quell suspicion that someone other than Uriah is the father of the child. But Uriah is too noble to go home while his fellow soldiers are at war, and he spends the night guarding the king's palace. So, after being convinced that he could not whitewash his sin through deception, David has recourse to murder. Sending a message to his commander in the field, David instructs him to place Uriah in the thick of the fight in order to be killed by the enemy. Finally, it is reported to David that Uriah is dead. Now David is free to take the dead man's wife. Uriah shines in this narrative as a superb moral exemplar over and against the wretched David.

Sin upon sin—self-absorption, abuse of power, adultery, deception, murder—David has used his royal power to conceal his intentions and decisions. But the despicable series of wrongs has unfolded under the watchful eye of God. There is a king more powerful even than David, someone whom David cannot manipulate or intimidate. So, the King of kings sends his prophet Nathan to David with a case of injustice between two men—one rich, the other poor—to the required royal intervention (verse 1).

Nathan tells his parable in such a way that it describes the reality of David's condition with discomforting accuracy. In relating the account of the rich man taking the beloved lamb of the poor man, Nathan makes the rich man appear not only unjust but remarkably self-absorbed. He appeals to David's moral responsibility for the weakest among his subjects. The prophet has marvelously set his trap, for David's anger is stirred: "As the Lord lives, the man who has done this deserves to die; he shall restore the lamb fourfold, because he did this thing, and because he had no pity" (verses 5–6). David has accurately identified lack of compassion as the precipitating offence.

With the trap sprung, Nathan delivers his devastating jolt, "You are the man!" (verse 7). The king remains utterly submissive as the prophet lays out the implications of David's sins. He had everything he could have wanted, yet he "despised the word of the Lord," committing adultery and murder (verses 8–9). Although David had been able to fool his fellow Israelites, he could not deceive the Lord, who sees not only the actions of history but also the movements of the heart. This episode is the turning point in the story of David's reign. Violence and adultery will relentlessly arise within his own family, demonstrating the awful truth that violence by its nature gives rise to violence, and betrayal generates betrayal (verses 10–11). Our wrongs have a ripple effect around us in all directions.

To David's everlasting credit, upon hearing the charge and its consequences, he admits his guilt: "I have sinned against the Lord" (verse 13). David is still willing to cast himself on God's mercy. He knows well that Israel's Torah dictates that he should be put to death for his crime. But because of his confession and repentance, David is allowed to live and to begin again: "Now the Lord has put away your sin; you shall not die." Although the consequences of his sin are grave, including the death of their child, David receives the undeserved grace of forgiveness.

It is remarkable that the Bible contains this account of King David's fall into sin. The story of the hero in most any other culture would omit a scene as embarrassing for the hero as this one. David is one of Israel's finest: slayer of

Goliath, friend to Jonathan, loyal servant of Saul, anointed of God, and man after God's own heart. Yet he sinned. And because he acknowledged his sin and repented, God forgave him. David continues to be remembered as Israel's greatest king. But following his sin and repentance and following his child's death, he no longer behaves with egocentric resolve, relying on his own cunning. He acts, rather, with vulnerability and detachment. His reign over Israel continues, and God's promises to his royal lineage remain.

Reflection and discussion

- Why did Nathan confront David with a parable instead of just a direct accusation of his sin?

- Do I allow people to confront me with my wrongdoing? How do I usually respond when confronted with something I have done wrong?

- What are some of the consequences of David's sin as spoken by Nathan? Why does the choice to do wrong bring inevitable consequences?

Prayer

King of kings, who sends prophets to confront rulers and trouble the consciences of the powerful, guide people into my life to confront me with my sin. Shatter my self-centered life and make me vulnerable and reliant on your grace.

"Hear in heaven your dwelling place their prayer and
their plea, maintain their cause and forgive your people
who have sinned against you, and all their transgressions
that they have committed against you." 1 KINGS 8:49–50

Solomon Pleads for God to Forgive Israel's Sin

1 KINGS 8:30–40, 46–50 ³⁰*"Hear the plea of your servant and of your people
Israel when they pray toward this place; O hear in heaven your dwelling place;
heed and forgive.*

³¹*"If someone sins against a neighbor and is given an oath to swear, and comes
and swears before your altar in this house,* ³²*then hear in heaven, and act, and
judge your servants, condemning the guilty by bringing their conduct on their
own head, and vindicating the righteous by rewarding them according to their
righteousness.*

³³*"When your people Israel, having sinned against you, are defeated before an
enemy but turn again to you, confess your name, pray and plead with you in this
house,* ³⁴*then hear in heaven, forgive the sin of your people Israel, and bring them
again to the land that you gave to their ancestors.*

³⁵*"When heaven is shut up and there is no rain because they have sinned against
you, and then they pray toward this place, confess your name, and turn from their
sin, because you punish them,* ³⁶*then hear in heaven, and forgive the sin of your servants, your people Israel, when you teach them the good way in which they should*

walk; and grant rain on your land, which you have given to your people as an inheritance.

[37]*"If there is famine in the land, if there is plague, blight, mildew, locust, or caterpillar; if their enemy besieges them in any of their cities; whatever plague, whatever sickness there is;* [38]*whatever prayer, whatever plea there is from any individual or from all your people Israel, all knowing the afflictions of their own hearts so that they stretch out their hands toward this house;* [39]*then hear in heaven your dwelling place, forgive, act, and render to all whose hearts you know—according to all their ways, for only you know what is in every human heart—*[40]*so that they may fear you all the days that they live in the land that you gave to our ancestors.*

[46]*"If they sin against you—for there is no one who does not sin—and you are angry with them and give them to an enemy, so that they are carried away captive to the land of the enemy, far off or near;* [47]*yet if they come to their senses in the land to which they have been taken captive, and repent, and plead with you in the land of their captors, saying, 'We have sinned, and have done wrong; we have acted wickedly';* [48]*if they repent with all their heart and soul in the land of their enemies, who took them captive, and pray to you toward their land, which you gave to their ancestors, the city that you have chosen, and the house that I have built for your name;* [49]*then hear in heaven your dwelling place their prayer and their plea, maintain their cause* [50]*and forgive your people who have sinned against you, and all their transgressions that they have committed against you; and grant them compassion in the sight of their captors, so that they may have compassion on them."*

King Solomon, the son of David, is best remembered for building the temple in Jerusalem, the centerpiece of his reign. The First Book of Kings has led up to this prayer of Solomon, offered at the temple's dedication. He prays that God will heed the prayers of the Israelites in their times of need and forgive their wrongdoing.

Although Solomon has said to God, "I have built you an exalted house, a place for you to dwell in forever" (8:13), Solomon begins his prayer by specifying that the temple is not a place for God to actually live: "Will God indeed dwell on the earth? Even heaven and the highest heaven cannot contain you, much less this house that I have built" (8:27). God dwells in heaven, but Solomon and the people will pray in this place where God has said, "My name shall be there" (verse 29). Solomon prays that God keep his eyes "open night and day toward this house."

Solomon emphasizes both the nearness and the transcendence of God as he beseeches God to respond to Israel's prayers: "O hear in heaven your dwelling place; heed and forgive" (verse 30). In each petition, Solomon implores God to "hear in heaven" (verses 32, 34, 36, 39). Yet, each appeal is prayed either "in" the temple (verses 31, 33) or "toward" the temple (verses 35, 38, 48). If the people are not in Jerusalem and therefore unable to offer prayer in the temple, then they must turn in the direction of the temple from wherever they are.

The petitions of Solomon's prayer describe a series of crises in which Israel will need to petition God's attention in the future. These include judicial cases, defeat in battle, drought, famine, plague, siege, sickness, and, finally, captivity in the land of an enemy—a rough preview of the trials that Israel will face during the centuries of its monarchy. In each situation, the people must repent, turning away from whatever hinders their devotion to God and turning toward God with faith and loving obedience.

The temple served as Israel's mediator between heaven and earth. The people prayed in the direction of the temple, and God responded to their prayers from his dwelling in heaven. Through the temple and the sacrifices offered there, God's forgiveness was offered to his people. God was sacramentally present with Israel through worship in the temple, yet even heaven itself could not contain creation's God. Ultimately Israel's living temple is Jesus the Messiah. The one who dwells in heaven has come to earth.

Solomon's final appeal to God refers to Israel's captivity in the land of their exile (verses 46–50). Yet, during Israel's captivity by the Babylonians, the temple in Jerusalem was razed to the ground. The people continued to pray in the direction of the demolished temple and hoped for its rebuilding. Solomon implores the people to admit their sin and repent with all their heart and soul, seeking God's forgiveness. The repentance that will end Israel's exile is a turning toward the temple. Since, for Christians, Jesus is the living temple, when God's people pray through him, with him, and in him, they can be confident that their sins are forgiven and they can become forgivers of others.

Reflection and discussion

- In what ways does Solomon emphasize both the nearness and the transcendence of God as he dedicates the temple? How do I experience both aspects of God's presence?

- Why did Solomon enjoin the people to pray toward the temple? In what direction do I pray to God?

- What was the role of the temple in seeking God's forgiveness? Why is Jesus described as the new temple who forgives the offenses of his people?

Prayer

O Lord, God of Israel, there is none like you in heaven above or on earth beneath. Hear my plea when I cry out to you. Forgive my sins as I turn away from whatever hinders my devotion to you and turn toward you in confident trust.

SUGGESTIONS FOR FACILITATORS, GROUP SESSION 2

1. If there are newcomers who were not present for the first group session, introduce them now.

2. You may want to pray this prayer as a group:
   Faithful and redeeming God of Israel, who is merciful and gracious to the thousandth generation, in every age you have given your people ways to repair human failures and to maintain their covenant with you. As you have pardoned the iniquity, transgressions, and sins of your people, forgive our failures to trust in your promises. Through the transforming power of your word, make us aware of how vulnerable we are and how much we rely on your grace.

3. Ask one or more of the following questions:
   - What was your biggest challenge in Bible study over this past week?
   - What did you learn about God's love from your study this week?
   - What did you learn about yourself this week?

4. Discuss lessons 1 through 6 together. Assuming that group members have read the Scripture and commentary during the week, there is no need to read it aloud. As you review each lesson, you might want to briefly summarize the Scripture passages of each lesson and ask the group what stands out most clearly from the commentary.

5. Choose one or more of the questions for reflection and discussion from each lesson to talk over as a group. You may want to ask group members which question was most challenging or helpful to them as you review each lesson.

6. Keep the discussion moving, but don't rush the discussion in order to complete more questions. Allow time for the questions that provoke the most discussion.

7. Instruct group members to complete lessons 7 through 12 on their own during the six days before the next group meeting. They should write out their own answers to the questions as preparation for next week's group discussion.

8. Conclude by praying aloud together the prayer at the end of lesson 6, or any other prayer you choose.

**I said, "I will confess my transgressions to the Lord,"
and you forgave the guilt of my sin.** PSALM 32:5

A Song of Confession and Forgiveness

PSALM 32

¹*Happy are those whose transgression is forgiven,*
whose sin is covered.
²*Happy are those to whom the Lord imputes no iniquity,*
and in whose spirit there is no deceit.
³*While I kept silence, my body wasted away*
through my groaning all day long.
⁴*For day and night your hand was heavy upon me;*
my strength was dried up as by the heat of summer. Selah
⁵*Then I acknowledged my sin to you,*
and I did not hide my iniquity;
I said, "I will confess my transgressions to the Lord,"
and you forgave the guilt of my sin. Selah
⁶*Therefore let all who are faithful*
offer prayer to you;
at a time of distress, the rush of mighty waters
shall not reach them.
⁷*You are a hiding place for me;*
you preserve me from trouble;
you surround me with glad cries of deliverance. Selah

⁸I will instruct you and teach you the way you should go;
   I will counsel you with my eye upon you.
⁹Do not be like a horse or a mule, without understanding,
   whose temper must be curbed with bit and bridle,
   else it will not stay near you.
¹⁰Many are the torments of the wicked,
   but steadfast love surrounds those who trust in the Lord.
¹¹Be glad in the Lord and rejoice, O righteous,
   and shout for joy, all you upright in heart.

The psalm begins with a blessing on those who experience the forgiveness of God. Whether wrongdoing is described as transgression, sin, iniquity, or deceit, happiness is experienced when the offense is pardoned so that life is not characterized by deception (verses 1–2). The psalm teaches the consequences of refusing to acknowledge sins, the importance of confessing offenses to God, and the blessedness of forgiveness. It instructs others based on what the psalmist has learned from his own experience of repentance, confession, and forgiveness.

The psalmist testifies that his refusal to admit his sins to God caused great physical and emotional distress (verses 3–4). The cause of his anguish was not so much his sin but his "silence" about his sin and his attempts to hide it. The psalmist knew full well how he had turned away from God by his transgression, and he knew that God also fully knew this. But, as a result of pride or fear, he refused to confess his sin to God, to acknowledge that he had done wrong, and to come before God asking for forgiveness.

The psalm then contrasts "I kept silence" with "I acknowledged my sin to you, and I did not hide my iniquity" (verse 5). When, at last, the psalmist is able to admit his wrong and confess his sin, God forgives him. His burden is lifted. Instead of needing to avoid the thought of God, he can now turn to God, trusting God as his refuge and source of strength.

The divine-human dynamic of confession and forgiveness is also the pattern for our relationships with others. When one has wronged a spouse, parent, neighbor, or friend, and refused to acknowledge it, the wrong hardens and diminishes the relationship. The offense can be dealt with only when it is put into words and spoken about. The same pattern applies to relationships between individuals and between communities. A wrong, when it is retained and sheltered, becomes part of one's identity.

Confession of sin must be made honestly and with integrity. God cannot be deceived, but sinners may deceive themselves by relying only on self-help, holding secret regret, and harboring guilt. Forgiveness is an act of divine grace. God always desires to forgive, but we must remove the obstacles to that forgiveness by admitting our sins to God. Our confession cannot be routine, shallow, or a means of cheap grace. Rather, it must be our means of growing in holiness.

Paul quotes the first two verses of this psalm in his teachings on God's graciousness (Romans 4:7–8). Attributing the psalm to King David, Paul suggests that any number of laudable things could be said of David, but none of them could make up for his sins. His "happiness" is due to the fact that the forgiveness of his sins comes from an act of God's grace. Through this psalm, Paul explains that the happiness of those who experience God's forgiveness is the result of trusting in God and in the work of Christ. Those who turn to God and away from sin must look not to their own righteousness but to the crucified Christ as God's judgment on our sins and as God's forgiveness of our guilt.

Reflection and discussion

- What is some of the physical, mental, emotional, and spiritual distress caused by refusal to confess wrongs and seek forgiveness?

- In what ways am I "like a horse or a mule, without understanding, whose temper must be curbed with bit and bridle" (verse 9) when I refuse to trust in God?

- Why must wrongdoing be put into words and spoken aloud in order for forgiveness and healing to occur?

- How does confessing my sins to God aid me in deepening my relationships with those I love?

Prayer

Merciful Lord, who is always ready to forgive, help me to recognize my wrongs and acknowledge my offenses. Let no deceit be found within me as I admit my transgressions, turn to you, and receive your gracious forgiveness.

Wash me thoroughly from my iniquity, and cleanse me from my sin.
For I know my transgressions, and my sin is ever before me.
PSALM 51:2–3

Pleading for the Grace of Forgiveness

PSALM 51

¹Have mercy on me, O God,
    according to your steadfast love;
according to your abundant mercy
    blot out my transgressions.
²Wash me thoroughly from my iniquity,
    and cleanse me from my sin.
³For I know my transgressions,
    and my sin is ever before me.
⁴Against you, you alone, have I sinned,
    and done what is evil in your sight,
so that you are justified in your sentence
    and blameless when you pass judgment.
⁵Indeed, I was born guilty,
    a sinner when my mother conceived me.
⁶You desire truth in the inward being;
    therefore teach me wisdom in my secret heart.
⁷Purge me with hyssop, and I shall be clean;
    wash me, and I shall be whiter than snow.

⁸*Let me hear joy and gladness;*
  let the bones that you have crushed rejoice.
⁹*Hide your face from my sins,*
  and blot out all my iniquities.
¹⁰*Create in me a clean heart, O God,*
  and put a new and right spirit within me.
¹¹*Do not cast me away from your presence,*
  and do not take your holy spirit from me.
¹²*Restore to me the joy of your salvation,*
  and sustain in me a willing spirit.
¹³*Then I will teach transgressors your ways,*
  and sinners will return to you.
¹⁴*Deliver me from bloodshed, O God,*
  O God of my salvation,
  and my tongue will sing aloud of your deliverance.
¹⁵*O Lord, open my lips,*
  and my mouth will declare your praise.
¹⁶*For you have no delight in sacrifice;*
  if I were to give a burnt offering, you would not be pleased.
¹⁷*The sacrifice acceptable to God is a broken spirit;*
  a broken and contrite heart, O God, you will not despise.
¹⁸*Do good to Zion in your good pleasure;*
  rebuild the walls of Jerusalem,
¹⁹*then you will delight in right sacrifices,*
  in burnt offerings and whole burnt offerings;
  then bulls will be offered on your altar.

This great penitential prayer has been ascribed in Israel's tradition to King David, Scripture's greatest penitent, who said to God, "I have sinned greatly in that I have done this thing. But now, I pray you, take away the guilt of your servant" (1 Chronicles 21:8). Through its association with this dark period of David's life, this psalm presents a poetic reflection on the nature of his sin and his forgiveness. The power of this magnificent prayer is proven by the fact that it was chanted for centuries in the temple of

Jerusalem and retains a prominent place in the liturgical life of the Christian church through the ages.

Although the psalmist tries to remain silent and keep his sin concealed, the wrong causes him great distress: "For I know my transgressions, and my sin is ever before me" (verse 3). His sin stares him in the face. Because he is one of God's holy ones, he knows he is a sinner. Like so many other characters in Scripture who encounter the living God, he is painfully aware of his own sinfulness and his unworthiness to come into God's holy presence.

The opening verses offer several synonyms for wrongdoing: transgressions, iniquity, and sin (verses 1–2). Likewise, several different metaphors describe the process of forgiveness: blotting out, thoroughly washing, and cleansing from sin. Through these words and images, the sinner humbly acknowledges his wrong and asks for God's merciful forgiveness.

The psalmist acknowledges that our being is disordered and prone to sin (verses 4–5). From conception and birth, every person is immersed in the sin of humanity. So the problem is not just the need to be pardoned for a particular wrong but to be delivered from the predicament of my being. God's will as the criteria for human acts reveals wrongdoing to be not only an offense against other people but a sin against God. For this reason, all of God's judgments and verdicts are thoroughly just.

The psalmist knows that his renewal will not come just from his own efforts to change, but from God working deep within him. He prays, "You desire truth in the inward being; therefore teach me wisdom in my secret heart" (verse 6). Rather than a change of situation, the psalmist knows that he needs an inner transformation. He prays that he may be re-created: "Create in me a clean heart, O God, and put a new and right spirit within me" (verse 10). In the Bible, "create" is an act that can be done only by God. What is said of the "heart" and "spirit" characterizes the condition and direction of a person's life. A clean heart and a right spirit designate a mind and will oriented to God, true to God's covenant, and ready to offer praise.

The psalmist's vocabulary of forgiveness and re-creation is the ritual language of worship: purging with hyssop and washing with water (verse 7). They are external actions that express an inward transformation. Yet, it is not the action itself, the sacrifice or burnt offering, that pleases God (verses 16–17). Rather, the broken spirit and contrite heart that the sacrifice symbolically represents is the offering that God accepts. The humble heart and spirit designate the mind and will turned to God, that knows it belongs to God, that offers itself to God.

The restoration of the city of Jerusalem (verses 18–19) completes the transformation of God's people. Both the restored city and the renewed people are the result of God's forgiveness. In the transformed Jerusalem, inhabited by a people with clean hearts and right spirits, the ritual worship of God can resume in a way that is in harmony with God's design. The continual chanting of this psalm from repentant hearts expresses the praise of a joyful and forgiven people.

Reflection and discussion

- What are some of the elements of repentance and forgiveness expressed in this psalm?

- How can my worship become more pleasing to God in light of this psalm?

Prayer

O God of my salvation, who forgave the sins of David your servant, create in me a clean heart and a right spirit. May I offer you the living sacrifice of a life offered to you, living in your covenant and giving you praise.

If you, O Lord, should mark iniquities, Lord, who could stand?
But there is forgiveness with you, so that you may be revered.
PSALM 130:3–4

Waiting with Confidence in the Lord's Forgiveness

PSALM 130

¹*Out of the depths I cry to you, O Lord.*
    ²*Lord, hear my voice!*
Let your ears be attentive
    to the voice of my supplications!
³*If you, O Lord, should mark iniquities,*
    Lord, who could stand?
⁴*But there is forgiveness with you,*
    so that you may be revered.
⁵*I wait for the Lord, my soul waits,*
    and in his word I hope;
⁶*my soul waits for the Lord*
    more than those who watch for the morning,
    more than those who watch for the morning.
⁷*O Israel, hope in the Lord!*
    For with the Lord there is steadfast love,
    and with him is great power to redeem.
⁸*It is he who will redeem Israel*
    from all its iniquities.

Crying to God "out of the depths" means imploring the Lord from the watery deep, overwhelmed by turbulent waters, sucked into chaos, and drowning in confusion (verse 1). The depths are as far away from God as one can get, the distance the psalmist has created by his own sinfulness, and thus, it is an apt image for severe distress. The psalmist is making a desperate effort to draw God's attention to his plight and receive a hearing (verse 2).

The psalmist contrasts an erroneous understanding of God and its consequences for the human condition (verse 3) with the truth about God and its significance for the human condition (verse 4). The error is an understanding of the Lord as one who keeps an eye out for human iniquities and keeps track of all our sins. The rhetorical question, "If you, O Lord, should mark iniquities, Lord, who could stand?" strips us of pride because we have plenty of iniquities, but it also relieves us of the pressure of trying to be something we are not. All people stand as sinners before God, and none would survive if this were God's way.

Instead, the psalm teaches the truth that the Lord's way toward us is forgiveness. God has both the authority and the desire to forgive our iniquities. The psalmist praises God with confidence: "But there is forgiveness with you, so that you may be revered." The human predicament is the flood of wrongs and their consequences, from which we cannot escape. The sinfulness of humanity sweeps us into the depths. In this inescapable predicament, we depend on God's forgiving grace to rescue us.

The result of God's pardon is that God may be "revered" by us. God does not just overlook our sin; his forgiveness is not automatic. God forgives so that, as a result, we might have a reverent and trusting relationship with the Lord whose way is mercy.

The psalm provides the appropriate stance for those sinking in a sea of iniquity: "I wait for the Lord, my soul waits, and in his word I hope" (verse 5). Waiting on the Lord with hope is the way to escape the flood of sin and be rescued by God. This is hope that is the result of God's word, the divine promises that offer strength in times of trouble. It is hope that will not be discouraged in the midst of struggle.

Thus, the imagery of the psalm moves from a frantic cry from the depths, a desperate plea for God to listen, to a gentle image of waiting for the Lord, like "those who watch for the morning" (verse 6). The lovely phrase is repeated twice as the poet contemplates the tender image of waiting in confident trust for the dawn.

The psalmist's own experience has embodied both the guilt and the hope of Israel. In the closing verses, the psalmist addresses the congregation directly, urging them to put their "hope in the Lord" (verses 7–8). Like the psalmist, the whole community must wait in hope, trusting that they will experience God's forgiveness, faithful love, and merciful redemption.

Reflection and discussion

- How do I determine whether or not something is worth the wait?

- With what attitude does the psalmist await forgiveness (verses 5–6)?

- When have I experienced the movement from crying "out of the depths" to a confident "hope in the Lord"?

Prayer

God of unfailing love, whose mercy lasts from age to age, in you I place my hope for forgiveness. Help me to await your pardon with confident trust, watching for the dawn of redemption.

**Though your sins are like scarlet, they shall be like snow;
though they are red like crimson, they shall become like wool.**

ISAIAH 1:18

Isaiah Exhorts Contrition for Social Sin

ISAIAH 1:15–20

¹⁵*When you stretch out your hands,*
I will hide my eyes from you;
even though you make many prayers,
I will not listen;
your hands are full of blood.
¹⁶*Wash yourselves; make yourselves clean;*
remove the evil of your doings
from before my eyes;
cease to do evil,
¹⁷learn to do good;
seek justice,
rescue the oppressed,
defend the orphan,
plead for the widow.
¹⁸*Come now, let us argue it out,*
says the Lord:
though your sins are like scarlet,
they shall be like snow;

though they are red like crimson,
    they shall become like wool.
[19]If you are willing and obedient,
    you shall eat the good of the land;
[20]but if you refuse and rebel,
    you shall be devoured by the sword;
    for the mouth of the Lord has spoken.

ISAIAH 6:1–8 [1]In the year that King Uzziah died, I saw the Lord sitting on a throne, high and lofty; and the hem of his robe filled the temple. [2]Seraphs were in attendance above him; each had six wings: with two they covered their faces, and with two they covered their feet, and with two they flew. [3]And one called to another and said:

"Holy, holy, holy is the Lord of hosts;
    the whole earth is full of his glory."

[4]The pivots on the thresholds shook at the voices of those who called, and the house filled with smoke. [5]And I said: "Woe is me! I am lost, for I am a man of unclean lips, and I live among a people of unclean lips; yet my eyes have seen the King, the Lord of hosts!"

[6]Then one of the seraphs flew to me, holding a live coal that had been taken from the altar with a pair of tongs. [7]The seraph touched my mouth with it and said: "Now that this has touched your lips, your guilt has departed and your sin is blotted out." [8]Then I heard the voice of the Lord saying, "Whom shall I send, and who will go for us?" And I said, "Here am I; send me!"

Isaiah's vision in the temple of Jerusalem profoundly changes both his inner and outer life. He sees God enthroned in royal garments amidst his heavenly court (6:1–2). This is the king who rules all the earth and all of history. The six-winged seraphim attending God's throne praise the holiness of God. This divine holiness is the dominant quality of God throughout Isaiah's prophecies. The threefold proclamation, "Holy, holy, holy is the Lord of hosts," is the Hebrew superlative: God alone is most holy (6:3). The "glory" that fills "the whole earth" is God's visible splendor made known in creation. The song probably reflects an ancient liturgical acclamation chanted in the temple.

The proclamation of God's holiness, which shook the temple and filled it with smoke, awed Isaiah and made him aware of his own unholiness and unworthiness (6:4–5). Although he fears the holiness of God in the face of his own shamefulness, he learns that holiness can mean forgiveness. The Lord who is "high and lofty" (6:1) also cares for the lowly and dishonorable. Merciful grace and forgiveness belong just as much to the essence of God's holiness as purity and sanctity. Symbolizing the prophet's forgiveness, the seraph touched the flaming coal to Isaiah's lips saying, "Your guilt has departed and your sin is blotted out" (6:7). With lips cleansed and his life purified, God's prophet is now ready to hear God's call and respond with ready service: "Here I am; send me!" (6:8).

Isaiah proclaims, as do the other prophets, that sacrifice and prayer are unacceptable to God when they are offered by those who have no concerns for the rights and needs of other people (1:15). To those who close their eyes and ears to oppression and the needs of orphans and widows, God will hide his eyes and will not listen. The hands that are stretched out to God are full of the blood of violence and injustice.

The prophet follows with a rhetorical torrent of imperatives: wash, remove, cease, learn, seek, rescue, defend, plead (1:16–17). Because God abhors the sacrifices and prayers of those who oppress the helpless members of society, Isaiah calls his listeners to a conversion of mind and heart. They are responsible for getting the blood off their own hands and giving up the evil deeds that stand shamefully before God's eyes. They must learn to do good for others and to seek justice. When their deeds are in sync with their faith, they will know the Lord's merciful forgiveness.

As in a court case, God challenges his people, "Come now, let us argue it out" (1:18). God offers them the choice of blessings or the sword, to "eat the good of the land" or to "be devoured" by their enemies (1:19–20). God offers them forgiveness, but it comes as their choice. Forgiveness is not a cheap or easy grace. The bloody scarlet and crimson of their sins will become like snow and wool, if they are "willing and obedient," conforming their lives to God's word and covenant.

Reflection and discussion

- In what ways did Isaiah's vision change his inner and outer life?

- How does God's forgiveness enable me, like Isaiah, to hear and respond to God's call to serve?

- Why does God refuse to see and hear the sacrifices and prayers of his people? What is God's condition for their forgiveness?

Prayer

Holy, holy, holy is the Lord of hosts. Heaven and earth are full of your glory. Cleanse me of my sin and let me experience your holiness as forgiveness. Accept my offering as I seek to do good and to act justly.

**I will cleanse them from all the guilt
of their sin against me, and I will forgive all the guilt
of their sin and rebellion against me.**
JEREMIAH 33:8

God Will Forgive
Their Iniquity

JEREMIAH 31:31–34 *³¹The days are surely coming, says the Lord, when I will make a new covenant with the house of Israel and the house of Judah. ³²It will not be like the covenant that I made with their ancestors when I took them by the hand to bring them out of the land of Egypt—a covenant that they broke, though I was their husband, says the Lord. ³³But this is the covenant that I will make with the house of Israel after those days, says the Lord: I will put my law within them, and I will write it on their hearts; and I will be their God, and they shall be my people. ³⁴No longer shall they teach one another, or say to each other, "Know the Lord," for they shall all know me, from the least of them to the greatest, says the Lord; for I will forgive their iniquity, and remember their sin no more.*

JEREMIAH 33:6–9 *⁶I am going to bring [Jerusalem] recovery and healing; I will heal them and reveal to them abundance of prosperity and security. ⁷I will restore the fortunes of Judah and the fortunes of Israel, and rebuild them as they were at first. ⁸I will cleanse them from all the guilt of their sin against me, and I will forgive all the guilt of their sin and rebellion against me. ⁹And this city shall be to me a name of joy, a praise and a glory before all the nations of the earth who shall hear* *of all the good that I do for them; they shall fear and tremble because of all the good and all the prosperity I provide for it.*

The prophet Jeremiah, speaking in the days after the Babylonians had defeated the kingdom of Judah and destroyed the city of Jerusalem, declares an oracle of hope in a period when the future seems lost. God's people has broken the covenant, the intimate relationship that God had established with them since the exodus from Egypt and the divine encounter at Mount Sinai (31:32). This covenant was like an intimate spousal bond, with God as "their husband" and the people as God's bride. But the covenant is now broken because of the guilt of the people's sin and rebellion against God. The Babylonians had destroyed the temple and deported the king, bringing an end to the priesthood and monarchy, the two most tangible expressions of God's presence with his people.

Into this desperate state, Jeremiah issues an optimistic message: God is going to bring "recovery and healing" to his espoused people (33:6). God is going to "restore" and "rebuild" the people, reuniting the divided southern kingdom of Judah and the northern kingdom of Israel (33:7). God will "cleanse" and "forgive" them of "all the guilt of their sin and rebellion" (33:8). This divine forgiveness will bring joy, praise, glory, good, and prosperity to the city of Jerusalem (33:9). The fulfillment of this hopeful oracle is the messianic future for God's people after the time of exile.

In these days that are "surely coming," God will establish a "new covenant" with his reunited people (31:31). This covenant will be radically different from that made by God with Israel at Mount Sinai. This broken covenant will not result in permanent divorce, but with a restoration of the spousal relationship. God desires repentance from his people and is ready to forgive those who turn away from sin and toward uprightness. Through the power of divine love, God says, "I will forgive their iniquity, and remember their sin no more" (31:34). The fact that God will not remember the sins of his people does not mean that God will erase his memory of them. Rather, it means that God will not treat them as though they are sinners.

The first covenant is not annulled; rather, it is renewed, intensified, and expanded. All will know the Lord, "from the least to the greatest." This new covenant will be written, not on stone, but on the hearts of God's people. In this way, it will be an unbreakable relationship, a covenant of which God will declare, "I will be their God, and they shall be my people." Israel will know God and desire God's ways from their inmost selves because God will wondrously change the heart of his people with divine grace (31:33). Indeed, this is a radically new kind of covenant.

The New Testament teaches that the roles of king and priest, lost in the exile, are restored, renewed, and perfected with Jesus Christ. He inaugurated a new and everlasting covenant on the eve of his death, as he gave the cup to his disciples with these words: "This cup that is poured out for you is the new covenant in my blood" (Luke 22:20). The new king and new priest offered the perfect sacrifice on the cross and offered his blood for the forgiveness of sins. With this new covenant, the prophecies are fulfilled, and all people, from the least to the greatest, will come to know the Lord with a rightly directed heart.

Reflection and discussion

• Why is divine forgiveness of all the guilt of the people's sin and rebellion against God so essential for a renewed covenant?

• Why is it helpful to consider God's covenant as a spousal relationship with his people?

- In what ways is the new covenant a renewal and expansion of the old covenant?

- What does the forgiveness of God do to the hearts of his people?

- How can God's forgiving grace lead to the healing of broken and struggling relationships?

Prayer

Divine Healer, who taught your people to await a new covenant, transform my heart so that I may experience a deeper desire to know you and to respond to your will. Accept my repentance as I receive your new and everlasting covenant.

"O Lord, hear; O Lord, forgive; O Lord, listen and act
and do not delay! For your own sake, O my God,
because your city and your people bear your name!"
DANIEL 9:19

Daniel Pleads for the Lord's Forgiveness

DANIEL 9:4–19 ⁴*I prayed to the Lord my God and made confession, saying,*

"Ah, Lord, great and awesome God, keeping covenant and steadfast love with those who love you and keep your commandments, ⁵we have sinned and done wrong, acted wickedly and rebelled, turning aside from your commandments and ordinances. ⁶We have not listened to your servants the prophets, who spoke in your name to our kings, our princes, and our ancestors, and to all the people of the land.

⁷*"Righteousness is on your side, O Lord, but open shame, as at this day, falls on us, the people of Judah, the inhabitants of Jerusalem, and all Israel, those who are near and those who are far away, in all the lands to which you have driven them, because of the treachery that they have committed against you. ⁸Open shame, O Lord, falls on us, our kings, our officials, and our ancestors, because we have sinned against you. ⁹To the Lord our God belong mercy and forgiveness, for we have rebelled against him, ¹⁰and have not obeyed the voice of the Lord our God by following his laws, which he set before us by his servants the prophets.*

¹¹*"All Israel has transgressed your law and turned aside, refusing to obey your voice. So the curse and the oath written in the law of Moses, the servant of God, have been poured out upon us, because we have sinned against you. ¹²He has con-*

firmed his words, which he spoke against us and against our rulers, by bringing upon us a calamity so great that what has been done against Jerusalem has never before been done under the whole heaven. [13]*Just as it is written in the law of Moses, all this calamity has come upon us. We did not entreat the favor of the Lord our God, turning from our iniquities and reflecting on his fidelity.* [14]*So the Lord kept watch over this calamity until he brought it upon us. Indeed, the Lord our God is right in all that he has done; for we have disobeyed his voice.*

[15]*"And now, O Lord our God, who brought your people out of the land of Egypt with a mighty hand and made your name renowned even to this day—we have sinned, we have done wickedly.* [16]*O Lord, in view of all your righteous acts, let your anger and wrath, we pray, turn away from your city Jerusalem, your holy mountain; because of our sins and the iniquities of our ancestors, Jerusalem and your people have become a disgrace among all our neighbors.* [17]*Now therefore, O our God, listen to the prayer of your servant and to his supplication, and for your own sake, Lord, let your face shine upon your desolated sanctuary.* [18]*Incline your ear, O my God, and hear. Open your eyes and look at our desolation and the city that bears your name. We do not present our supplication before you on the ground of our righteousness, but on the ground of your great mercies.* [19]*O Lord, hear; O Lord, forgive; O Lord, listen and act and do not delay! For your own sake, O my God, because your city and your people bear your name!"*

The prophet Daniel prays aloud this liturgical prayer of confession and penitence in the name of the people. He and the people of Judah know that their future does not lie in the hands of the imperial powers that have conquered them, but in God alone. They stand before God as sinful people, yet confidently as a community that God has claimed as his own.

Daniel addresses God who is "great and awesome," faithful in "keeping covenant and steadfast love" (verse 4). In contrast, the prophet relentlessly confesses the guilt of God's people, acknowledging that the destruction of Jerusalem was deserved punishment for the people's sins. He loads five largely synonymous terms into one verse: we have "sinned," "done wrong," "acted wickedly," "rebelled," and "turned aside" from God's commandments (verse 5). Built within the workings of the covenant is the certain assurance that violation of the commands inscribed in the Torah brings about the covenant curses. Rebellion against God's will has inevitable consequences which God's people have experienced.

Daniel offers no excuses or mitigating circumstances. The prayer moves back and forth between acknowledging the uprightness of God and the sin of the people. Daniel prays, "Righteousness is on your side, O Lord" (verse 7), but "Open shame, O Lord, falls upon us" (verse 8). To God belongs "mercy and forgiveness" (verse 9), but God's people have not obeyed the voice of the Lord (verse 10). According to Israel's theology, guilt is inescapably followed by punishment. Because Israel transgressed God's covenant, "the curse and the oath written in the law of Moses, the servant of God, have been poured out upon us" (verse 11).

With the pivotal phrase "And now," the prayer moves from the confession of past sins to the long-awaited appeal to God's mercy (verse 15). Addressing God as Israel's deliverer, the Lord who brought his people out of Egypt, Daniel prays that God let his anger "turn away" from Jerusalem (verse 16). Although God's people were unable to turn away from their iniquities, they petition God to turn away his wrath from them. In a second pivot, "Now therefore," Daniel asks God to "listen" to the prayer of his people who refused to "listen" to God (verse 17). The prayer is remarkable in that Israel can continue to petition God, though their sin would seem to have disqualified them completely.

The prayer continues with a flurry of imperatives, calling upon God to respond to the prayers of his people: "listen," "let your face shine," "incline your ear and hear," "open your eyes and look" (verses 17–18). Israel's many failures are contrasted with God's "great mercies." The possibility of Israel's reconciliation with God and a new future rests completely in God's generosity as his people throw themselves upon his faithful love.

The final verse has been called Daniel's *Kyrie eleison*. A threefold call, "O Lord," is accompanied by an appeal for God to hear, forgive, listen, and act (verse 19). The appeal is made not only to God's mercy, but also to God's self-interest. Daniel asks God to forgive Israel "for your own sake." He urges God to act "because your city and your people bear your name." Surely God would not abandon what is his own. Because God has chosen Jerusalem and the people of Israel as his own, Daniel can pray this bold prayer. God's people can hope for an end to their suffering and a new beginning because of God's merciful and faithful love toward his own. It is an incredibly daring act to pray in this way after such a profound confession of sin. Yet Daniel can do so because he knows that God's honor and glory is deeply linked to Israel's future. And for Israel to have a future, God must be willing to relinquish the past and forgive his people.

Reflection and discussion

- Why does Daniel consider it important to confess the sins of God's people before asking for God's help?

- Why is confessing my sins good for me?

- What could happen if I began the daily practice of self-examination: reviewing my day, becoming aware of omissions and failings, confessing them to God, and calling upon the transforming power of God's merciful love?

Prayer

O Lord, our God, who keeps your covenant in faithfulness, I confess that I have sinned and turned aside from your commands. I plead for your forgiveness, not because of my worthiness, but because of your great mercy.

SUGGESTIONS FOR FACILITATORS, GROUP SESSION 3

1. Welcome group members and ask if there are any announcements anyone would like to make.

2. You may want to pray this prayer as a group:

   God of unfailing love, whose mercy lasts from age to age, with the psalmists we turn to you. Acknowledging our sin, we admit our wrongs and plead for your mercy. With the prophets, we confess that we have turned aside from your will and ask your forgiveness. Through your transforming grace, renew us from the inside out, creating a clean heart within us so that we may offer you the living sacrifice of our lives. As we watch for the dawn of your redemption, help us to do good and to act justly.

3. Ask one or more of the following questions:
   - Which message of Scripture this week speaks most powerfully to you?
   - What is the most important lesson you learned through your study this week?

4. Discuss lessons 7 through 12. Choose one or more of the questions for reflection and discussion from each lesson to discuss as a group. You may want to ask group members which question was most challenging or helpful to them as you review each lesson.

5. Remember that there are no definitive answers for these discussion questions. The insights of group members will add to the understanding of all. None of these questions require an expert.

6. After talking about each lesson, instruct group members to complete lessons 13 through 18 on their own during the six days before the next group meeting. They should write out their own answers to the questions as preparation for next week's group discussion.

7. Ask the group if anyone is having any particular problems with the Bible study during the week. You may want to share advice and encouragement within the group.

8. Conclude by praying aloud together the prayer at the end of one of the lessons discussed. You may add to the prayer based on the sharing that has occurred in the group.

"Whenever you stand praying, forgive, if you have anything against anyone; so that your Father in heaven may also forgive you your trespasses." MARK 11:25

Forgive Before Making an Offering to God

MARK 11:24–26 [24]*"So I tell you, whatever you ask for in prayer, believe that you have received it, and it will be yours.*

[25]*"Whenever you stand praying, forgive, if you have anything against anyone; so that your Father in heaven may also forgive you your trespasses. [*[26]*But if you do not forgive, neither will your Father in heaven forgive your trespasses."]*

MATTHEW 5:23–24 [23]*"So when you are offering your gift at the altar, if you remember that your brother or sister has something against you, *[24]*leave your gift there before the altar and go; first be reconciled to your brother or sister, and then come and offer your gift."*

Jesus teaches about the necessity of forgiveness in the context of his teachings on prayer. He first encourages his disciples to pray with single-mindedness and wholehearted trust in God (Mark 11:24). In addition, they must "forgive" if they want their prayer for personal forgiveness by God to be effective (Mark 11:25). Those who want to be forgiven of their "trespasses" must forgive those who have offended them.

Similar sayings of Jesus about the importance of forgiveness are found throughout the gospels. It seems certain that for Jesus and the evangelists, being forgiven by God and forgiving others cannot be separated. Here, in both the gospels of Mark and Matthew, Jesus is teaching that forgiving others must proceed God's forgiving us. But in other New Testament passages, our forgiveness of others follows God's forgiveness of us (Luke 7:41–43, 47; Ephesians 4:32; Colossians 3:13). What is clear throughout is that forgiving and being forgiven go hand in hand.

Mark 11:26 is not included in most contemporary versions of the gospel because it was not present in the most ancient manuscripts of the Greek text. This indicates that the words were probably added by an early copyist to clarify the teaching and to make it conform to Jesus' teaching in Matthew 6:14–15. Nevertheless, the teaching is from Jesus, as recorded by Matthew, even though Mark did not include it himself.

In Matthew's gospel, Jesus offers a concrete situation to demonstrate that personal reconciliation takes precedence over offering prayer and sacrifice in the temple (Matthew 5:23–24). Significantly, the situation here does not pertain to one's own trespasses but to the offenses of another: "If you remember that your brother or sister has something against you." So, disciples must not only forgive others but also initiate reconciliation with others who have offended them. It is not a question of who affronted whom but of taking personal responsibility to make the first move toward reconciliation.

This instruction in Matthew's gospel takes place within Jesus' Sermon on the Mount, a collection of teachings in which Jesus shows how his way fulfills the ancient Scriptures. He proclaims that he did not come to abolish the law of God but to fulfill it. As the definitive interpreter of the Torah, Jesus reveals the ultimate meaning of the law of God and brings it to its intended goal. Throughout the sermon, Jesus demonstrates how being forgiven by God, forgiving others, and seeking reconciliation with others form the heart of the Christian life.

It is easy for us to run through the laws of God, noticing that we have not killed anyone or stolen anything, giving ourselves a passing grade. But the examination of conscience that Jesus would have us perform cuts deeper and is far more thorough. He wants us to imitate God, seeking to love without limit and forgiving as God forgives.

Reflection and discussion

- What comes first in my experience: me forgiving others or God forgiving me? Why are these so closely related?

- Why does Jesus direct his followers to seek reconciliation before making an offering to God?

- Is it possible or reasonable to forgive as God forgives?

Prayer

Lord Jesus, who has called me to be your disciple and sent me out to live the good news of the kingdom, teach me to forgive and to seek forgiveness. Send your Spirit to examine my heart, showing me how to recognize my need to forgive.

"Give us this day our daily bread. And forgive us our debts, as we also have forgiven our debtors." MATTHEW 6:11–12

Learning to Pray for Forgiveness

MATTHEW 6:7–15 [7]*"When you are praying, do not heap up empty phrases as the Gentiles do; for they think that they will be heard because of their many words.* [8]*Do not be like them, for your Father knows what you need before you ask him.*

[9]*"Pray then in this way:*

Our Father in heaven,

hallowed be your name.

[10]*Your kingdom come.*

Your will be done,

on earth as it is in heaven.

[11]*Give us this day our daily bread.*

[12]*And forgive us our debts,*

as we also have forgiven our debtors.

[13]*And do not bring us to the time of trial,*

but rescue us from the evil one.

[14]*For if you forgive others their trespasses, your heavenly Father will also forgive you;* [15]*but if you do not forgive others, neither will your Father forgive your trespasses."*

As Jesus continues his Sermon on the Mount, he shows his disciples how to bring divine forgiveness into the context of prayer. Because prayer is rooted in an intimate relationship with God, forgiveness from God is essential. Guilt hardens personal barriers into solid walls, obstructing our intimacy with God. On the other hand, forgiveness softens barriers so that they dissolve.

Jesus describes the internal disposition that motivates true disciples at prayer, urging them to pray with open hearts to God rather than with elaborate display and empty words (verse 7). His instruction, "Pray then in this way," suggests that he is offering a model prayer, not just a prayer to be memorized but a pattern to follow in all of our prayer (verse 9). Addressing his prayer to "Our Father," Jesus invites us to share in his own prayer life, to participate in his intimate relationship with God, and to involve ourselves in the life of the Trinity. In the Holy Spirit, we can consider ourselves as children of God alongside Jesus.

In giving us a blueprint for our prayer, Jesus models a familial relationship with God and highlights the prayer of praise, contrition, and petition. The first three phrases, all of which contain the word "your," focus on God: "Hallowed be your name" asks that God's name be held in reverence; "Your kingdom come" prays that God complete his work of creation and redemption; and "Your will be done" asks that we strive to follow God's will as obediently as we can on earth, while realizing that God's desire for creation will only be accomplished when heaven and earth are one (verses 9–10).

The next three petitions, all of which contain the word "us," focus on our needs. While we hope for God's future kingdom, we pray for the practical and urgent needs we experience as we live in a world not yet fully conformed to God's will. These petitions ask God to help us with our human needs for sustenance, forgiveness, and strength in the face of testing and evil—in other words, they pray for provisions, pardon, and protection (verses 11–13). "Give us this day our daily bread" requests that God grant us the divine nourishment to sustain us in all aspects of our lives. "Forgive us our debts, as we also have forgiven our debtors" asks God to pardon the debts we create when we sin against God and others. Finally, "Do not bring us to the time of trial, but rescue us from the evil one" asks God to help us stand firm in the face of whatever testing, temptation, or enticement to sin comes our way.

The version of the Lord's Prayer in Matthew's gospel uses a financial metaphor, describing sin as a debt and forgiveness as the removal of a debt. This understanding of sin conveys the idea that we owe something to those we have wronged and need to pay them back so as to undo the harm that was done. But as sinners, we accumulate an increasing burden of debt that we cannot repay. We can only pray that God will take upon himself the burden that we owe, thus canceling our debt.

This understanding of sin reminds us that it costs a person something to forgive us. If we expect to be forgiven without also being willing to bear the cost of forgiving others, we introduce more injustice into the world. So as we pray that God forgive us, we cannot omit "as we also have forgiven our debtors." Thus, the forgiveness we invoke is not given without condition. If we forgive others their trespasses, we open our lives to experience the forgiveness of our heavenly Father (verse 14). However, if we are unwilling or unable to forgive others, we will be incapable of receiving the forgiveness of God.

The Lord's Prayer is the prayer of the church, of those who have received the comprehensive forgiveness of God that has become flesh in Jesus Christ. This incarnate forgiveness must now have its effects in everything we think and say and do. Our relationships with one another must be permeated by the fact that we live in God's forgiveness. If we refuse to forgive others or if we are unable to forgive, we make it known that we have not fully received this complete and inclusive forgiveness of God. When we truly accept this incarnate forgiveness in the flesh, so that it permeates our lives with the power to make new our whole way of life, then we can forgive those who trespass against us.

Reflection and discussion

- Pray the Lord's Prayer again, imagining the prayer coming directly from the heart and lips of Jesus himself. What do I particularly notice through this imaginative experience?

- Jesus describes sin as a debt and forgiveness as the removal of a debt. How does this affect my understanding of God's forgiveness of me and my need to forgive others?

- If I understand the Lord's Prayer as a model for my personal prayer, how can I renew or improve my prayer to God?

- Why does forgiving others help me to experience my Father's forgiveness more fully in my own life?

Prayer

Incarnate Lord, who embodies the forgiveness of the Father, help me to develop a heart like your own and to pray in the way you taught me. Help me to accept the divine forgiveness you have offered to the world.

"So that you may know that the Son of Man has authority on earth to forgive sins"—he then said to the paralytic—"stand up, take your bed and go to your home." MATTHEW 9:6

The Authority to Heal and Forgive

MATTHEW 9:2–8 *²And just then some people were carrying a paralyzed man lying on a bed. When Jesus saw their faith, he said to the paralytic, "Take heart, son; your sins are forgiven." ³Then some of the scribes said to themselves, "This man is blaspheming." ⁴But Jesus, perceiving their thoughts, said, "Why do you think evil in your hearts? ⁵For which is easier, to say, 'Your sins are forgiven,' or to say, 'Stand up and walk'? ⁶But so that you may know that the Son of Man has authority on earth to forgive sins"—he then said to the paralytic—"Stand up, take your bed and go to your home." ⁷And he stood up and went to his home. ⁸When the crowds saw it, they were filled with awe, and they glorified God, who had given such authority to human beings.*

The gospels present many demonstrations of Jesus' power to heal, but here Jesus wants to lead his followers to a deeper understanding of his authority. His words to the paralytic, "Take heart, son; your sins are forgiven," are not what the man or those carrying him were expecting to hear (verse 2). But Jesus, evidently seeing deeply into the man's heart, knows that forgiveness is his greatest need. Sin is an illness more dangerous than physical sickness. Guilt is a paralysis that prevents us from coming to the Lord.

For this man, forgiveness is the precondition for his being healed from his enslaving disability.

There is a widespread tendency to blame sickness on sin, and some have even suggested that Jesus connected this man's disability with his sinfulness. But this is not what the account is demonstrating. Jesus does not say that the man's sin is the cause of his infirmity. In fact, in other places throughout the gospels, Jesus challenges the notion that human suffering is the result of sin. For example, when encountering the man who was born blind, Jesus denies that the sin of the man or his parents caused him to be blind from birth (John 9:2–3). Although there is no causal link between individual illness and personal sin, there is certainly a connection between healing and forgiveness. In fact, modern science continually discovers more links between emotional wholeness and physical well-being, joining the body and spirit for holistic health.

Some of the scribes assume that Jesus, by claiming the divine prerogative to forgive sins, is speaking blasphemy, a serious charge punishable by death (verse 3). But in response to their suspicions, Jesus asks them, "Which is easier, to say, 'Your sins are forgiven,' or to say, 'Stand up and walk'?" (verse 5). It seems easier to speak the words of divine forgiveness because forgiveness cannot be outwardly displayed, whereas words of healing require an immediate demonstration. So, in order to prove to them that he has authority to absolve sins, Jesus does what is "harder" as a sign of his authority to do what seems "easier." The walking paralytic returning home to begin a new life is a visible demonstration that "the Son of Man has authority on earth to forgive sins" (verse 6).

We know nothing about the man before his healing, and after his healing we still know nothing, except that "he stood up and went to his home" (verse 7). We'd like to know more about what forgiveness did for this man. Yet Matthew wants to show us only who Jesus is. Although Jesus had become known as a healer, he claimed for himself the ability to forgive sins. As great as his power is to heal the sick, it pales in comparison to his authority over sin. In Jesus, the very power of God was present on earth. Although sick people may be healed, they will inevitably get sick again, and ultimately they will die. Sin is at the root of all human struggles with evil, and Jesus' power to overcome the effects of sin is the heart of his mission.

Reflection and discussion

- Why didn't Jesus simply heal the physical disability of the man like the people were expecting?

- In what ways can sin and guilt paralyze people? Why is forgiveness often a prerequisite for true healing?

- What might be some of the connections between bodily healing and spiritual forgiveness in human experience?

Prayer

Healing Lord, you know the deepest need of my heart, and you desire my healing in body and soul. Give me the ability to trust in you and to experience your power to forgive my sins.

"Whoever speaks a word against the Son of Man will be forgiven, but whoever speaks against the Holy Spirit will not be forgiven, either in this age or in the age to come." MATTHEW 12:32

The Unforgivable Blasphemy

MATTHEW 12:22–32 ²²*Then they brought to him a demoniac who was blind and mute; and he cured him, so that the one who had been mute could speak and see.* ²³*All the crowds were amazed and said, "Can this be the Son of David?"* ²⁴*But when the Pharisees heard it, they said, "It is only by Beelzebul, the ruler of the demons, that this fellow casts out the demons."* ²⁵*He knew what they were thinking and said to them, "Every kingdom divided against itself is laid waste, and no city or house divided against itself will stand.* ²⁶*If Satan casts out Satan, he is divided against himself; how then will his kingdom stand?* ²⁷*If I cast out demons by Beelzebul, by whom do your own exorcists cast them out? Therefore they will be your judges.* ²⁸*But if it is by the Spirit of God that I cast out demons, then the kingdom of God has come to you.* ²⁹*Or how can one enter a strong man's house and plunder his property, without first tying up the strong man? Then indeed the house can be plundered.* ³⁰*Whoever is not with me is against me, and whoever does not gather with me scatters.* ³¹*Therefore I tell you, people will be forgiven for every sin and blasphemy, but blasphemy against the Spirit will not be forgiven.* ³²*Whoever speaks a word against the Son of Man will be forgiven, but whoever speaks against the Holy Spirit will not be forgiven, either in this age or in the age to come."*

On one occasion in the gospels, Jesus speaks of the possibility that God will not forgive sin. This statement seems totally contrary to all of Jesus' other teachings, proclaiming God's readiness to forgive all those who repent. In this troublesome saying, Jesus speaks of something on the human side that would make divine forgiveness impossible. In order to understand this so-called "unforgivable sin," it must be examined in its context.

When Jesus cures the blind and mute man who was possessed by a demon, a conflict arose over the source of his power. The crowds are amazed at his power and wonder whether Jesus is the Messiah, while the Pharisees view his power not as messianic but demonic (verses 23–24). They accuse Jesus of acting in the power of Beelzebul, the ruler of the demons.

The response of Jesus uses images to illustrate the absurdity of their claim that Satan is using Jesus to cast out the very demons Satan sent to possess people. First, he states that a "kingdom" at war with itself cannot survive and that a "city or house" cannot last when divided by internal strife (verse 25). Likewise, if Satan casts out Satan, his kingdom is divided against itself and cannot stand (verse 26). And since the Pharisees also practice exorcism, Jesus accuses their argument of being inconsistent—they slander Jesus for doing the same thing they do (verse 27). Instead, Jesus teaches that the true power behind his saving work is the Spirit of God (verse 28). The same Holy Spirit active in the conception of Jesus (Matt 1:18) and empowering him for ministry since his baptism (Matt 3:16) now indicates that the kingdom of God has arrived.

With a second image, Jesus explains the real strategy of his saving work against the powers of evil. He compares Satan to a strong man guarding his house and property (verse 29). Those over whom Satan has possession cannot be released until the strong man is tied with ropes and his house plundered. Jesus is breaking into the domain of evil, binding the power of Satan, wrecking his property, and freeing his captives from his tyrannical rule.

Jesus concludes his encounter with the Pharisees with both a statement of hope and a solemn warning. First, Jesus assures his listeners that God will forgive all sins and blasphemies anyone may commit, thus affirming the unlimited mercy of God (verse 31). Then Jesus cautions, "Blasphemy against the Spirit will not be forgiven." In attributing the work of Jesus to the spirit of evil, the Pharisees defiantly deny the action of the Holy Spirit working through Jesus. In this way they refuse to accept God's mercy, erecting a permanent barrier between themselves and God. Without the interior guidance and divine grace provided by God's Spirit, repentance and faith are impossible.

What is the difference between speaking "against the Son of Man," which is forgivable, and speaking "against the Holy Spirit," which will not be forgiven? God's mercy is so inclusive that even those who insult and reject Jesus, out of ignorance, obstinacy, or fear, can be forgiven. But those who willfully reject the work of the Holy Spirit refuse to accept God's healing mercy and cannot be forgiven. There is no single act of which one could not repent and be forgiven, thus no single act can qualify as blasphemy against the Holy Spirit. It refers, rather, to a mindset that refuses to believe in sin, that rejects any need to repent, that denies any hope for human transformation. Although God offers forgiveness to everyone, no matter what their sin, refusing to acknowledge that anything needs to be forgiven means remaining unforgiven.

Reflection and discussion

- What is blasphemy against the Holy Spirit? Why is it the only sin that cannot be forgiven?

- When have I been tempted to blaspheme the Holy Spirit?

- What are the indications that the reign of Satan has been bound and his captives set free?

- In what sense is "the unforgivable sin" a mindset rather than a single act?

- How much do I acknowledge my need for God's mercy and my desire for God's forgiveness?

Prayer

Messiah and Lord, who casts out the powers of evil and brought the kingdom of God to us, save us from sin and heal us in your mercy through the power of the Holy Spirit.

**"Lord, if another member of the church sins against me,
how often should I forgive? As many as seven times?"**
MATTHEW 18:21

Forgive Ceaselessly

MATTHEW 18:21–35 ²¹*Then Peter came and said to him, "Lord, if another member of the church sins against me, how often should I forgive? As many as seven times?" ²²Jesus said to him, "Not seven times, but, I tell you, seventy-seven times.*

²³*"For this reason the kingdom of heaven may be compared to a king who wished to settle accounts with his slaves. ²⁴When he began the reckoning, one who owed him ten thousand talents was brought to him; ²⁵and, as he could not pay, his lord ordered him to be sold, together with his wife and children and all his possessions, and payment to be made. ²⁶So the slave fell on his knees before him, saying, 'Have patience with me, and I will pay you everything.' ²⁷And out of pity for him, the lord of that slave released him and forgave him the debt. ²⁸But that same slave, as he went out, came upon one of his fellow slaves who owed him a hundred denarii; and seizing him by the throat, he said, 'Pay what you owe.' ²⁹Then his fellow slave fell down and pleaded with him, 'Have patience with me, and I will pay you.' ³⁰But he refused; then he went and threw him into prison until he would pay the debt. ³¹When his fellow slaves saw what had happened, they were greatly distressed, and they went and reported to their lord all that had taken place. ³²Then his lord summoned him and said to him, 'You wicked slave! I forgave you all that debt because you pleaded with me. ³³Should you not have had mercy on your fellow slave, as I had mercy on you?' ³⁴And in anger his lord handed him over to be tortured until he would pay his entire debt. ³⁵So my heavenly Father will also do to every one of you, if you do not forgive your brother or sister from your heart."*

In asking Jesus about the extent of forgiveness within the community of believers, Peter assumes that surely it is adequate to offer forgiveness seven times to an offender. Jesus' answer, however, indicates that forgiveness must be ceaseless (verse 22). His response, "seventy-seven times," alludes to the response of Lamech, a descendant of Cain, who boasts that he will exact overwhelming vengeance on anyone who dares attack him: "If Cain is avenged sevenfold, truly Lamech seventy-sevenfold" (Genesis 4:24). Jesus presents forgiveness as the complete reverse of revenge. Disciples must renounce the instinct to retaliate against someone who repeatedly wrongs them and offer unlimited forgiveness.

Jesus then offers a parable to illustrate the importance of forgiving others and the consequences of refusing to forgive. The impact of the parable is found in the contrast between the huge debt owed by the slave, a massive amount that could never possibly be repaid, and the comparatively small debt owed to the slave. The parable's effect is found next in the contrast between the king's deeply emotional and bighearted decision to forgive the slave's debt completely and that same slave's brutal and merciless response to his fellow slave. He hypocritically accepts pardon but is unwilling to grant it to another. Because the slave has already been forgiven an astounding and unpayable obligation by his king, the generosity he received ought to flow over into his relationship with others. He should live the rest of his life in memory of that amazing grace he received.

This illustration of Jesus' teaching shows us that we must be constant in our forgiving because God's forgiving mercy toward us knows no bounds. Each of us is that slave who owed a staggering amount, but whose debt was pardoned by the merciful king. If such a debt has been forgiven for us by God, how generous should we be in forgiving others? Peter's question addresses a human problem from a human perspective. This parable of the kingdom grounds forgiveness in the very nature of God.

The compassion of the king (verse 27) forms a strong contrast with the king's revoking his forgiveness and punishing the unforgiving slave (verses 32–34). The images of severe punishment reinforce the point of the parable and emphasize the consequences of failing to forgive as we have been forgiven. Ironically, the unforgiving slave is treated in the end as he treated his fellow slave. Thus, if we do not forgive those who have sinned against us, we break the gracious relationship God has established with us, and the sins we commit will remain unforgiven. In fact, the unforgiving slave will never be able to repay all that he owes to the king, suggesting the eternal consequences of refusing to forgive.

Unlimited forgiveness must not be confused with toleration of harmful behaviors. It cannot be misconstrued as condoning evil. We must not excuse violent or addictive behavior with a false kind of forgiveness. Wrong must be identified, challenged, and acknowledged as wrong and as requiring correction. Genuine forgiveness must lead to health and wholeness, both for individuals and within families and communities.

Jesus urges disciples to "forgive your brother or sister from your heart" (verse 35). Although we have been lovingly forgiven by our God, we can only open our lives to receive that forgiveness when we forgive others from our hearts. As we forgive one another, we allow that tremendous forgiveness of God to take hold of our lives and renew us from within. When we have truly received the incarnate forgiveness of God, made known in Jesus Christ, when our hearts are thereby transformed by God's forgiving love, we are able to forgive from our heart. God's forgiveness then overflows from our lives into Christ's church. Those wishing to be part of this community and share in the kingdom must imitate the incalculable generosity and compassion of its Lord.

Reflection and discussion

- Is God's forgiveness conditional or unconditional? Why did the king not forgive the slave again if forgiveness must be limitless?

- What have I learned about forgiveness from the parable of Jesus?

- Why is forgiveness important both for the psychological health of individuals and for the health of families and communities?

- How do I decide if and when to forgive another?

Prayer

Lord Jesus, through your merciful grace, you ask me to overcome my natural instincts to seek revenge. Make me so grateful for your forgiveness that I let it overflow to others no matter the cost to me.

"Drink from it, all of you; for this is my blood of the covenant,
which is poured out for many for the forgiveness of sins."
MATTHEW 26:27–28

Poured Out for the Forgiveness of Sins

MATTHEW 26:26–29 ²⁶*While they were eating, Jesus took a loaf of bread, and after blessing it he broke it, gave it to the disciples, and said, "Take, eat; this is my body." ²⁷Then he took a cup, and after giving thanks he gave it to them, saying, "Drink from it, all of you; ²⁸for this is my blood of the covenant, which is poured out for many for the forgiveness of sins. ²⁹I tell you, I will never again drink of this fruit of the vine until that day when I drink it new with you in my Father's kingdom."*

In the words and gestures of the Last Supper, Jesus expresses the meaning of his own death and gives his church the means of renewing and making present again his own sacrificial offering on the cross. The "blood of the covenant" is drawn from Exodus 24, which narrates God's ratification of the covenant with Israel sealed in the blood of sacrifice. This blood of Jesus, which is poured out in his death on the cross, becomes the blood bond between God and the community of God's people. His words over the cup affirm that his death is the ultimate redeeming act "for the forgiveness of sins," liberating humanity from its most powerful bondage.

In the dying and rising of Christ, the ancient covenant is renewed and completed, fulfilling Jeremiah's prophecy of a new covenant which God's people await (Jeremiah 31:31–34). "The days are surely coming," Jeremiah had said. This new covenant would bring an internalizing of Israel's Torah: "I will put my law within them, and I will write it on their hearts." The climax of that prophetic promise was "I will forgive their iniquity and remember their sin no more."

Jeremiah spoke his prophetic word of the Lord in a desperate time, when the future seemed hopeless and the temple and priesthood had been destroyed. God's people had broken the covenant, the intimate bond that God had established with them since the exodus from Egypt and the divine encounter at Mount Sinai. But into this desperate state, Jeremiah issued a message of hope. Thus says the Lord: "I will cleanse them from all the guilt of their sin against me, and I will forgive all the guilt of their sin and rebellion against me" (Jeremiah 33:8). The fulfillment of this hopeful oracle is the messianic future for God's people after the time of exile.

Now Jesus is announcing to God's people that the time has come. With the shedding of his blood, the day of divine forgiveness has arrived and the new covenant is being enacted. The fulfillment of Jeremiah's words in the sacrifice of Christ shows that the "forgiveness of sins" accomplished in the pouring out of Christ's "blood of the covenant" is a complete kind of forgiveness. It not only pardons the past but overcomes the human inability to avoid sinning. It defeats the powers that cause people to turn toward evil, empowering them to internalize God's will and seek what is truly good.

This is a radically new kind of covenant that is renewed every time the church gathers for Eucharist. The temple and priesthood, lost in the exile, is restored and perfected in Christ. The new priest offers the perfect sacrifice and gives his blood for the forgiveness of sins. In the body and blood of Christ, given to us to eat and drink, we become the people of God in the fullest possible way. In the Eucharist, we come to know God and desire God's will from our inmost selves, because God is wondrously transforming our hearts to be like that of his Son.

The first covenant is not annulled; rather, it is renewed, intensified, and expanded. With this new covenant, all people from the least to the greatest will come to know the Lord with a rightly directed heart (Jeremiah 31:34). By sharing the Eucharist, we partake in the age-old forgiveness of our God: looking back to the covenant ratified at Mount Sinai in sacrificial blood, sharing in the "forgiveness of sins" made present in the blood of Christ, and anticipating that day when Christ will drink the fruit of the vine and share in the eternal banquet with us in the Father's kingdom (verse 29).

Reflection and discussion

- In what ways does Jesus Christ complete and perfect the temple and priesthood of ancient Israel?

- How do we experience divine forgiveness when we participate in the Eucharist?

- How does the forgiveness I experience in Christ's new covenant lead me to interior, personal transformation?

Prayer

Crucified Redeemer, who unites us in the new and everlasting covenant, send forth your Holy Spirit so that your body and blood may be my source of eternal forgiveness and life.

SUGGESTIONS FOR FACILITATORS, GROUP SESSION 4

1. Welcome group members and ask if anyone has any questions, announcements, or requests.

2. You may want to pray this prayer as a group:

   Crucified and redeeming Lord, who invites us to be transformed through the grace of the Holy Spirit, show us how to accept the forgiveness you have offered to the world and how to recognize our need to forgive others. You know the deepest desires of our hearts, and you desire to heal us in body and spirit. Through the sacrament of your Eucharist, join us together in the new covenant and deepen your presence within us. Make us grateful for your forgiveness, help us to overcome our instincts to seek revenge, and teach us how to let your mercy overflow into the lives of others.

3. Ask one or more of the following questions:
   - What is the most difficult part of this study for you?
   - What insights stand out to you from the lessons this week?

4. Discuss lessons 13 through 18. Choose one or more of the questions for reflection and discussion from each lesson to discuss as a group. You may want to ask group members which question was most challenging or helpful to them as you review each lesson.

5. Keep the discussion moving, but allow time for the questions that provoke the most discussion. Encourage the group members to use "I" language in their responses.

6. After talking over each lesson, instruct group members to complete lessons 19 through 24 on their own during the six days before the next group meeting. They should write out their own answers to the questions as preparation for next week's session.

7. Ask the group what encouragement they need for the coming week. Ask the members to pray for the needs of one another during the week.

8. Conclude by praying aloud together the prayer at the end of one of the lessons discussed. You may choose to conclude the prayer by asking members to pray aloud any requests they may have.

> "I tell you, her sins, which were many, have been forgiven;
> hence she has shown great love. But the one to whom
> little is forgiven, loves little." LUKE 7:47

The Relationship of Forgiveness and Love

LUKE 7:36–50 ³⁶*One of the Pharisees asked Jesus to eat with him, and he went into the Pharisee's house and took his place at the table.* ³⁷*And a woman in the city, who was a sinner, having learned that he was eating in the Pharisee's house, brought an alabaster jar of ointment.* ³⁸*She stood behind him at his feet, weeping, and began to bathe his feet with her tears and to dry them with her hair. Then she continued kissing his feet and anointing them with the ointment.* ³⁹*Now when the Pharisee who had invited him saw it, he said to himself, "If this man were a prophet, he would have known who and what kind of woman this is who is touching him—that she is a sinner."* ⁴⁰*Jesus spoke up and said to him, "Simon, I have something to say to you." "Teacher," he replied, "speak."* ⁴¹*"A certain creditor had two debtors; one owed five hundred denarii, and the other fifty.* ⁴²*When they could not pay, he canceled the debts for both of them. Now which of them will love him more?"* ⁴³*Simon answered, "I suppose the one for whom he canceled the greater debt." And Jesus said to him, "You have judged rightly."* ⁴⁴*Then turning toward the woman, he said to Simon, "Do you see this woman? I entered your house; you gave me no water for my feet, but she has bathed my feet with her tears and dried them with her hair.* ⁴⁵*You gave me no kiss, but from the time I came in she has not stopped kissing my feet.* ⁴⁶*You did not anoint my head with oil, but she has anointed my feet with ointment.* ⁴⁷*Therefore, I tell you, her sins, which were* *many, have been forgiven; hence she has shown great love. But the one to whom little is forgiven, loves little." ⁴⁸Then he said to her, "Your sins are forgiven." ⁴⁹But those who were at the table with him began to say among themselves, "Who is this who even forgives sins?" ⁵⁰And he said to the woman, "Your faith has saved you; go in peace."*

Jesus had gained a reputation for eating with all kinds of people, including tax collectors and sinners, so his acceptance of the invitation of Simon the Pharisee to dine in his home did not seem unusual. However, we discover that Simon's intentions were tainted because he does not offer Jesus the customary signs of hospitality. Ordinarily the host greeted his guests with a kiss. Servants would then wash the dust from the guests' feet and anoint their head with oil. Something seems amiss.

During the course of the meal, a woman of the city, who was known to be a sinner, makes an entrance (verse 37). Weeping profusely, she washes the feet of Jesus with her tears, dries them with her long, unbound hair, and kisses them with her lips. The smell of perfumed ointment fills the air as the woman pours from her alabaster jar of ointment, anointing the feet of Jesus. It becomes clear as the narrative continues that the woman and Jesus had met before, and that she has already experienced forgiveness as a result of his presence. Now, at the feet of Jesus, the woman expresses her gratitude to Jesus with extravagant gestures of love. Jesus says of her, "I tell you, her sins, which were many, have been forgiven; hence she has shown great love" (verse 47).

In response to the scene, Jesus draws a sharp contrast between Simon the Pharisee and the woman. Simon is not moved by the presence of Jesus in his home and does not even offer him the usual hospitality: washing his feet, greeting him with a kiss, and anointing him with oil (verses 44–46). The woman, on the other hand, is unrestrained in her displays of love because of her experience of forgiveness. Simon assesses the situation with nothing more than judgment—Jesus can't be a prophet; she's touching him; she's a sinner (verse 39). The woman, despite the judgment and the many stares in the room, knows that love is the only thing that matters.

Jesus, who is able to read the heart of Simon, tells a parable for his sake (verses 41–43). The point of the parable is so obvious that Simon cannot question it. A debtor whose great debt has been canceled responds with greater love to the creditor than a debtor who has been forgiven a much smaller amount. Thus, the woman who has been forgiven her many sins is appropriately extravagant in expressing her love for Jesus.

The powerful words of Jesus to the woman, "Your sins are forgiven," reassure her and also alert Simon and his other guests of Jesus' divine authority (verses 48–49). While the others express both amazement and suspicion, Jesus dismisses the woman with a blessing, "Your faith has saved you; go in peace." Salvation, a term of rescue from physical distress in the Old Testament, now refers to rescue from sin and its consequences. "Peace" is the wholeness and completeness that she is beginning to experience as a result of being forgiven. Her new life of salvation in Jesus brings her into a new relationship with God that transcends everything that had damaged that relationship in the past.

The scene teaches us that forgiveness allows us to love. The more we recognize our sinfulness and ask for God's forgiveness, the more we can receive mercy and experience love for God and others. The love that Jesus shows us in offering us forgiveness gives us the motivation and grace to love without counting the costs. When we accept the gift of forgiveness, we can love generously and lavishly.

Reflection and discussion

- What does Jesus see in this woman that Simon does not?

- What does Jesus seem to be trying to teach Simon in this account?

- What has the experience of forgiveness done for this woman with the alabaster jar?

- When has God's forgiveness freed me to love more generously?

Prayer

Merciful Lord, although I am a sinner, help me to experience your forgiveness. Give me the ability to love you lavishly and to share with others in the fruit of that love.

> "While he was still far off, his father saw him and was filled with compassion; he ran and put his arms around him and kissed him."
>
> LUKE 15:20

The Forgiving Father and His Two Sons

LUKE 15:11–32 [11]*Then Jesus said, "There was a man who had two sons.* [12]*The younger of them said to his father, 'Father, give me the share of the property that will belong to me.' So he divided his property between them.* [13]*A few days later the younger son gathered all he had and traveled to a distant country, and there he squandered his property in dissolute living.* [14]*When he had spent everything, a severe famine took place throughout that country, and he began to be in need.* [15]*So he went and hired himself out to one of the citizens of that country, who sent him to his fields to feed the pigs.* [16]*He would gladly have filled himself with the pods that the pigs were eating; and no one gave him anything.* [17]*But when he came to himself he said, 'How many of my father's hired hands have bread enough and to spare, but here I am dying of hunger!* [18]*I will get up and go to my father, and I will say to him, "Father, I have sinned against heaven and before you;* [19]*I am no longer worthy to be called your son; treat me like one of your hired hands."'* [20]*So he set off and went to his father. But while he was still far off, his father saw him and was filled with compassion; he ran and put his arms around him and kissed him.* [21]*Then the son said to him, 'Father, I have sinned against heaven and before you; I am no longer worthy to be called your son.'* [22]*But the father said to his slaves, 'Quickly, bring out a robe—the best one—and put it on him; put a ring on his finger and sandals on his feet.* [23]*And get the fatted calf and kill it, and let us eat* *and celebrate;* ²⁴*for this son of mine was dead and is alive again; he was lost and is found!' And they began to celebrate.*

²⁵*"Now his elder son was in the field; and when he came and approached the house, he heard music and dancing.* ²⁶*He called one of the slaves and asked what was going on.* ²⁷*He replied, 'Your brother has come, and your father has killed the fatted calf, because he has got him back safe and sound.'* ²⁸*Then he became angry and refused to go in. His father came out and began to plead with him.* ²⁹*But he answered his father, 'Listen! For all these years I have been working like a slave for you, and I have never disobeyed your command; yet you have never given me even a young goat so that I might celebrate with my friends.* ³⁰*But when this son of yours came back, who has devoured your property with prostitutes, you killed the fatted calf for him!'* ³¹*Then the father said to him, 'Son, you are always with me, and all that is mine is yours.* ³²*But we had to celebrate and rejoice, because this brother of yours was dead and has come to life; he was lost and has been found.'"*

For a son to ask his father to divide his property and give him his inheritance while his father still lives would be a terrible insult, tantamount to wishing his father's death. The younger son's request must have broken his father's heart. But the older son does not seem to protest the offense and takes his share too as the father "divided his property between them" (verse 12). That the younger son has fully rejected his home and family becomes clear as he sells the property and takes the proceeds with him to some distant land, where he then wastes all that he has (verse 13). But after spending carelessly and wastefully, the young man finds himself hungry and tired, longing for home.

While the regretful son is rehearsing what he will say to his father, we discover that the father has been watching and waiting for his return. When the father spots his son from afar, he runs to greet him, embracing and kissing him with joy. The gestures and emotions of the father create a scene of overwhelming love and forgiveness. It seems that the father's desire to forgive precedes and surpasses the son's desire to be forgiven. The son identifies himself with the stigma of his sins, but the father is bent on helping him reverse his shame-filled mindset. The fine robe, the ring, the sandals, and the feast of veal all proclaim the lost sinner as the father's beloved child.

Meanwhile, the older son has been working "in the field" (verse 25). He is the responsible one who has always done everything his father asked of him. When he hears the music and dancing, and then realizes that his father is celebrating the return of the younger son, he becomes angry and refuses to enter the house. But the father who ran toward one lost son now comes after the other one (verse 28). The older son complains, "For all these years I have been working like a slave for you, and I have never disobeyed your command" (verse 29). He is lost in his self-pity and bitter resentment, and he is unable to live the joyful life as a beloved child of his father.

Jesus addresses this parable to two groups who have drawn near to him: "the tax collectors and sinners," who are mirrored in the attitude of the younger son, and "the Pharisees and the scribes," who are mirrored in the mindset of the older son (15:1–2). Yet the parable is addressed to all the readers of the gospel. We are all lost children who have been found by our Father. Yet we maintain ways of thinking about God and relating to God that deprive us of joy in the Father's presence. Either we remain identified with our past sins and cannot accept that we are really sons and daughters, or we follow orders with obedience and can't believe that the Father's love is unmerited and free. Only when we accept our Father's unlimited grace with joy and gratitude can we truly celebrate and feel at home with God.

Reflection and discussion

- In what ways do the two sons express the attitudes of the sinners and the religious leaders?

- What do I see of myself in the mindset of each of the two sons?

- What does the father's responses to his two sons teach me about the nature of God?

- When have I seen God's forgiveness enable a person to leave behind a misguided past and begin a life transformed by hope and confidence?

Prayer

Compassionate Father, I have wandered from your care and become lost in selfishness. Give me the desire to turn back to you with all my heart so that I can experience your forgiveness and the joy of being at home with you.

"If the same person sins against you seven times a day, and turns back
to you seven times and says, 'I repent,' you must forgive."

LUKE 17:4

Jesus Forgives
His Persecutors

LUKE 17:3–4 ³"Be on your guard! If another disciple sins, you must rebuke the
offender, and if there is repentance, you must forgive. ⁴And if the same person
sins against you seven times a day, and turns back to you seven times and says,
'I repent,' you must forgive."

LUKE 23:32–43 ³²Two others also, who were criminals, were led away to be put
to death with him. ³³When they came to the place that is called The Skull, they
crucified Jesus there with the criminals, one on his right and one on his left. ³⁴Then
Jesus said, "Father, forgive them; for they do not know what they are doing." And
they cast lots to divide his clothing. ³⁵And the people stood by, watching; but the
leaders scoffed at him, saying, "He saved others; let him save himself if he is the
Messiah of God, his chosen one!" ³⁶The soldiers also mocked him, coming up and
offering him sour wine, ³⁷and saying, "If you are the King of the Jews, save yourself!" ³⁸There was also an inscription over him, "This is the King of the Jews."
  ³⁹One of the criminals who were hanged there kept deriding him and saying,
"Are you not the Messiah? Save yourself and us!" ⁴⁰But the other rebuked him,
saying, "Do you not fear God, since you are under the same sentence of condem-
nation? ⁴¹And we indeed have been condemned justly, for we are getting what

*we deserve for our deeds, but this man has done nothing wrong." *[42]*Then he said, "Jesus, remember me when you come into your kingdom." *[43]*He replied, "Truly I tell you, today you will be with me in Paradise."*

Luke's gospel emphasizes forgiveness throughout: from the beginning, when Zechariah's canticle proclaims God's message of "salvation to his people by the forgiveness of their sins" (1:77), to the end, when the disciples are told that "repentance and forgiveness of sins is to be proclaimed in his name to all the nations" (24:47). At the heart of Jesus' words and deeds is God's merciful forgiveness and the necessity of forgiving others.

When forgiveness is at the heart of people's relationships to one another, as it is in the community of Jesus' disciples, there is a quality in those relationships that allows people to also confront and rebuke one another without harming their bond. Thus, Jesus exhorts fellow disciples to reprimand one another about sin and to forgive one another upon repentance (17:3). Following Jesus is not a private affair; disciples are accountable to one another. Believers have a familial responsibility in community, helping others overcome their faults and move past their failures. So each time the request for forgiveness is made—even "seven times a day" by the same person— when repentance is genuine, it must be granted (17:4). Just as God's forgiveness is without limit, so must be that of the disciple.

The ultimate lesson in forgiveness is taught by Jesus from the cross. If Jesus had wanted to publicly condemn anyone to hell as a lesson for his followers, this would have been the moment to do so. Instead, he pleads for God's pardon for those who have thoroughly rejected him and are putting him to the most torturous death imaginable: "Father, forgive them" (23:34). He did not call down the fire of damnation on them; he made excuses for them: "For they do not know what they are doing."

Who are these whom Jesus asks the Father to forgive since they do not know what they are doing? Most responses to that question focus on the Roman soldiers, who are carrying out the orders of their superiors. What about the bystanders who mock Jesus, obviously enjoying their cruelty? What about Pilate, who was willing to condemn to a terrible death a man whom he decided was innocent of any crime? What about the religious leaders, who sought his death by falsely charging him with blasphemy? What about Peter, who denied Jesus, the other apostles, who failed in courage, or Judas, who betrayed him?

We don't know the mind of Jesus at this moment, nor do we know the heart of each of these people and whether they could accept God's forgiveness. But we can presume that Jesus' prayer to his Father from the cross is his ultimate example to his followers of all that he had taught them. He forgives even the unrepentant as an undeserved gift of divine grace. Jesus forgives his torturers, first of all, so that he would not enter death with any bitterness or resentment in his heart. And second, he forgives so that those who would repent might be restored and saved. How many of those who heard these words of Jesus from the cross were transformed to new life by his words of forgiveness? Luke tells us that the centurion praised God after seeing the manner of Jesus' death, and when the crowds saw what had taken place, they returned home, beating their breasts in repentance (23:47–48).

Only Luke's gospel recounts the exchange between the two criminals to the right and left of Jesus and the dialogue between the repentant criminal and Jesus. The repentant one highlights the innocence of Jesus in comparison with his own deeds, and he asks for a share in Jesus' kingdom. Emphasizing the forgiving effects of his own death for others, Jesus replies, "Truly I tell you, today you will be with me in Paradise" (23:43). This forgiven criminal is the crowning instance and result of Jesus' mission to call sinners to repentance and offer them forgiveness, to seek out and save the lost.

Reflection and discussion

- How does a spirit of mutual forgiveness enhance the quality of Christian community?

- How can I continually forgive without reinforcing bad behavior in another?

- Jesus' forgiveness of his persecutors from the cross shows us that even the worst of people can be redeemed. In what circumstances is it most difficult for me to forgive another?

- How does the forgiveness of Jesus on the cross alter my perception of people I am seeking to forgive?

Prayer

Crucified Lord, who gave your best teaching on forgiveness from the cross, teach me how to forgive those who do me harm. Help me to always trust in your merciful pardon so that I may be able to forgive those who offend me.

When they kept on questioning him, he straightened up and said to them, "Let anyone among you who is without sin be the first to throw a stone at her." JOHN 8:7

Neither Do I Condemn You

JOHN 8:2–11 *²Early in the morning [Jesus] came again to the temple. All the people came to him and he sat down and began to teach them. ³The scribes and the Pharisees brought a woman who had been caught in adultery; and making her stand before all of them, ⁴they said to him, "Teacher, this woman was caught in the very act of committing adultery. ⁵Now in the law Moses commanded us to stone such women. Now what do you say?" ⁶They said this to test him, so that they might have some charge to bring against him. Jesus bent down and wrote with his finger on the ground. ⁷When they kept on questioning him, he straightened up and said to them, "Let anyone among you who is without sin be the first to throw a stone at her." ⁸And once again he bent down and wrote on the ground. ⁹When they heard it, they went away, one by one, beginning with the elders; and Jesus was left alone with the woman standing before him. ¹⁰Jesus straightened up and said to her, "Woman, where are they? Has no one condemned you?" ¹¹She said, "No one, sir." And Jesus said, "Neither do I condemn you. Go your way, and from now on do not sin again."*

The scribes and Pharisees seem to have caught Jesus in an inescapable trap. The Romans did not allow the Jews to exact capital punishment, but the law of Moses, to which the accusers refer, prescribed death by stoning for anyone committing adultery. The woman's accusers state that she has been "caught in the very act of committing adultery" (verse 4).

They clearly have no real concern for the fate of the woman; they are out to get Jesus. Neither do they care about the injured husband or the partner in adultery, who has apparently gotten off scot-free. The Torah prescribes the death penalty for both the man and the woman involved (Leviticus 20:10; Deuteronomy 22:22–24). Concern for the woman was clearly not the issue for these men.

The drama is intense: the woman standing at the center encircled by the crowd, the adversaries ready to stone her, and all eyes on Jesus, to see what he will do next. Would Jesus oppose the civil authority or the religious law? As usual Jesus finds a third way.

The account unfolds in two parallel scenes, each beginning when Jesus bends down and writes on the ground (verses 6, 8). This gesture can be understood as a sign of the tranquil confidence of Jesus, who refuses to enter the zealous fervor of the woman's accusers. Refusing to address his challengers, he first chooses silence. Each time Jesus rises from the ground, he pronounces a pivotal verse of the narrative. He speaks first to the scribes and Pharisees about sin: "Let anyone among you who is without sin be the first to throw a stone at her" (verse 7). All remain silent as they recognize their own sinfulness and let go of their judgment. The accusers become the accused and gradually walk away.

When Jesus rises again from the ground, he is left alone with the woman and is the first person to speak to her directly. She is no longer an objective exhibit at a trial but a person who can enter into a personal encounter with Jesus. He does not judge or humiliate her. The forgiveness Jesus offers to her gives her the freedom to live a new life. Not only has Jesus saved her physical life from those who would stone her, but he also offers her the possibility of a genuine life in a right relationship with God (verse 11). The parting words of Jesus, "Go your way, and from now on do not sin again," acknowledge the woman's sinfulness but send her forth, filled with renewed hope.

The final scene reminds us of the forgiveness and freedom we experience when we admit our own sinfulness to the Lord. It presents Jesus as a merciful judge—the kind of judge we would wish to face at our own final judgment. Whenever we approach the throne of God's grace, sinful and sorrowful, we are not turned away the same as we came. He caresses the wounds caused by our sins. Divine forgiveness sends us on our way with new freedom, ready to begin again. Each experience of God's mercy calls us to deeper conversion and renewed faith.

Reflection and discussion

- What difference has it made when I have chosen silence before speaking?

- What happens when I read the account again, imagining myself as one of the religious officials, filled with righteous anger at a wrong gone unpunished? What changes inside of me as I drop my stone?

- From what types of imprisonment does Jesus free both the woman and the religious officials?

Prayer

Merciful Lord, who frees your people and offers them hope, help me to realize the depths of my sin and the liberation you offer through your forgiveness. Continue to transform my life with your healing grace.

He breathed on them and said to them, "Receive the Holy Spirit.
If you forgive the sins of any, they are forgiven them;
if you retain the sins of any, they are retained."

JOHN 20:22–23

The Ministry of Forgiveness

JOHN 20:19–23 ¹⁹*When it was evening on that day, the first day of the week, and the doors of the house where the disciples had met were locked for fear of the Jews, Jesus came and stood among them and said, "Peace be with you." ²⁰After he said this, he showed them his hands and his side. Then the disciples rejoiced when they saw the Lord. ²¹Jesus said to them again, "Peace be with you. As the Father has sent me, so I send you." ²²When he had said this, he breathed on them and said to them, "Receive the Holy Spirit. ²³If you forgive the sins of any, they are forgiven them; if you retain the sins of any, they are retained."*

When the disciples were trying to protect themselves behind locked doors, the risen Jesus appears in their midst. They are moved from a state of fear to the experience of joy and wonderment. The Lord's greeting, "Peace be with you" (verses 19, 21), is a common Hebrew salutation. Yet, hearing these words on the lips of Jesus who suffered and died, the one whom they deserted before his crucifixion, gives them a new richness. Peace (in Hebrew, *shalom*) is not just the absence of conflict; it is an experience of deep confidence that dispels fear and is full of hope.

Hearing these words from Jesus dispels their shame and offers them the freedom to envision a new future.

After his first greeting of peace, Jesus shows his hands and his side to his disciples. These wounds of suffering and victory convince the disciples that the risen one is not a phantom but the same Jesus who was lifted up on the cross. His wounds have become part of his identity as savior and redeemer. After his second greeting of peace, Jesus sends his disciples on their mission: "As the Father has sent me, so I send you." Because God so loved the world, he sent his Son to reveal the Father for all to see—through his teachings, his healing signs, and finally through his total self-gift on the cross. Now Jesus sends his chosen disciples on that same mission—to be for the world what he has been for the world—to embody the Father's love, to teach and heal, to comfort and bring peace, to love as Jesus has loved.

To empower the disciples to carry out this mission, Jesus breathes on them and says, "Receive the Holy Spirit" (verse 22). The breath of Christ, the empowering Spirit of God, enables the church to be for the world what Jesus has been for the world. Just as the Father has sent out Jesus in the power of the Holy Spirit, so now Jesus sends out his disciples in the power of that divine Spirit. Much as the Creator breathed life into the first human beings (Genesis 2:7) or as Ezekiel prophesied to the "breath" to revive the dry bones of his vision (Ezekiel 37:9), Jesus breathes his Spirit into God's new creation, the community of disciples empowered to forgive, heal, teach, and love in the name of the risen Christ.

At the core of the mission Jesus gives his community of disciples—to be for the world what he has been for the world—is the ministry of forgiveness. There is an inseparable relationship between receiving the Holy Spirit and engaging in practices of forgiveness. The Spirit enables those who have been forgiven in Christ to become those who forgive others. The words uttered by Jesus, "If you forgive the sins of any, they are forgiven them; if you retain the sins of any, they are retained," authorize the church to offer forgiveness of sins in the name of the risen Christ and in the power of the Holy Spirit. In cases where people are unwilling to demonstrate repentance, fellowship in the church may need to be temporarily suspended and the sin retained—but always as a remedial practice to encourage repentance and return to communion with the church.

Because the crucified Savior is risen, "the Lamb of God who takes away the sin of the world" (John 1:29) continues to forgive sins and retain sins through his church. The community of disciples, anointed with the Holy Spirit, bears the fruit of Jesus' victory to the world beyond the historical life of Jesus. In the midst of all the future fears and joys of God's people, the church will bring sanctification to generations of believers.

Reflection and discussion

- Why would the disciples be particularly joyful to hear the words "Peace be with you" from the lips of the risen Christ?

- What is the significance of the risen Christ showing his wounded hands and side to his disciples?

- Why did Jesus give the power to forgive sins to his church?

Prayer

Wounded Lord, risen to eternal life, let me know your peace in every part of my life. Empower me with your Spirit, and send me to offer your compassion, healing, and forgiveness to others.

Peter felt hurt because he said to him the third time, "Do you love me?" And he said to him, "Lord, you know everything; you know that I love you." Jesus said to him, "Feed my sheep."

JOHN 21:17

Peter Experiences the Lord's Forgiveness

JOHN 21:4–19 *⁴Just after daybreak, Jesus stood on the beach; but the disciples did not know that it was Jesus. ⁵Jesus said to them, "Children, you have no fish, have you?" They answered him, "No." ⁶He said to them, "Cast the net to the right side of the boat, and you will find some." So they cast it, and now they were not able to haul it in because there were so many fish. ⁷That disciple whom Jesus loved said to Peter, "It is the Lord!" When Simon Peter heard that it was the Lord, he put on some clothes, for he was naked, and jumped into the sea. ⁸But the other disciples came in the boat, dragging the net full of fish, for they were not far from the land, only about a hundred yards off.*

⁹When they had gone ashore, they saw a charcoal fire there, with fish on it, and bread. ¹⁰Jesus said to them, "Bring some of the fish that you have just caught." ¹¹So Simon Peter went aboard and hauled the net ashore, full of large fish, a hundred fifty-three of them; and though there were so many, the net was not torn. ¹²Jesus said to them, "Come and have breakfast." Now none of the disciples dared to ask him, "Who are you?" because they knew it was the Lord. ¹³Jesus came and took the bread and gave it to them, and did the same with the fish. ¹⁴This was now the third time that Jesus appeared to the disciples after he was raised from the dead.

15When they had finished breakfast, Jesus said to Simon Peter, "Simon son of John, do you love me more than these?" He said to him, "Yes, Lord; you know that I love you." Jesus said to him, "Feed my lambs." 16A second time he said to him, "Simon son of John, do you love me?" He said to him, "Yes, Lord; you know that I love you." Jesus said to him, "Tend my sheep." 17He said to him the third time, "Simon son of John, do you love me?" Peter felt hurt because he said to him the third time, "Do you love me?" And he said to him, "Lord, you know everything; you know that I love you." Jesus said to him, "Feed my sheep. 18Very truly, I tell you, when you were younger, you used to fasten your own belt and to go wherever you wished. But when you grow old, you will stretch out your hands, and someone else will fasten a belt around you and take you where you do not wish to go." 19(He said this to indicate the kind of death by which he would glorify God.) After this he said to him, "Follow me."

The final resurrection appearance of Jesus in John's gospel occurs back in Galilee. The disciples have returned home to resume their fishing trade after the brutal events of Christ's passion in Jerusalem. As the morning breaks, Jesus stands on the shore of the sea, but the disciples do not recognize him. Without him, they catch nothing, but with his direction, the catch is overwhelming (verse 6). The awe-inspiring catch of fish symbolically expresses the evangelizing mission Jesus has given to his disciples. The fishermen will now be catching men and women in their apostolic nets. The untorn net despite the abundant catch expresses the unity of the church for which Jesus has prayed.

The record-breaking catch is the catalyst for recognition. The beloved disciple displays insightful recognition and says to Peter, "It is the Lord!" (verse 7). Peter exhibits decisive action: he "jumped into the sea" in order to swim ashore to Jesus. The risen Lord has prepared breakfast for his disciples on the shore.

The "charcoal fire," upon which Jesus has placed cooked fish and bread, reminds us of the charcoal fire outside the high priest's house when Peter denied Jesus after his arrest (verse 9). But now, these burning coals by the sea roast a meal of reconciliation and communion. How different this fire must have looked to Peter in the light of dawn as the risen Lord invites the disciples to come and eat. The words and actions of Jesus echo his earlier meals with the loaves and fish and reflect the eucharistic meals of the church in which the disciples in every age encounter the risen Lord.

As Peter had three times denied his relationship with Jesus, now Jesus gives Peter this threefold opportunity to express his love for him (verses 15–17). Peter responds to the questions more cautiously this time, more humbly aware of his limitations and vulnerability. At long last, Peter has learned that he cannot follow Jesus in a way that relies on his own strength and willpower. Each of his affirmations of love offsets his earlier rejections. In the light of this new day, Peter's agonizing over his denials is brought to an end as he experiences the forgiving presence of the risen Lord.

Jesus' three questions lead to his entrusting Peter with the care of his flock. The triple commissioning expresses Peter's solemn obligation. The sheep, so precious to Jesus, are now given to the care of the sinful yet forgiven Peter. His responsibility implies total dedication to the community of faith, guidance through teaching and preaching, and self-giving even to the point of offering his life for them. In fact, Jesus follows his commission of Peter with a prediction of his death (verses 18–19). With his freedom taken away from him, Peter will be led to the place of his execution where he will stretch out his hands in crucifixion.

Jesus ends his commissioning of Peter with the same words that began his relationship: "Follow me." Only now Peter's call to follow Jesus takes on a fuller meaning. Repentant and forgiven, Peter will live in the shadow of the cross, reliant on God's saving grace. He will follow Jesus to the end, finally giving his life on the cross, and by his death, give glory to God.

Reflection and discussion

- How might the sight of the charcoal fire affect the memory and emotions of Peter? What does it symbolize in light of the resurrection?

- How did Peter's encounter with the risen Lord enable him to recover from his devastating denials?

- Why is Peter able to love Jesus more genuinely after his lakeside experience of forgiveness?

- What other qualities does Peter's repentance and forgiveness offer him for his apostolic leadership of Christ's church?

Prayer

Risen Lord, who forgave Peter for his threefold denial and called him to be shepherd of the church, manifest the healing power of your forgiveness throughout your church. May we follow you free from guilt and full of love.

SUGGESTIONS FOR FACILITATORS, GROUP SESSION 5

1. Welcome group members and ask if anyone has any questions, announcements, or requests.

2. You may want to pray this prayer as a group:
   Crucified and risen Lord, who forgave Peter on the seashore, the repentant thief on the cross, the remorseful woman caught in adultery, and the penitent woman who anointed your feet with perfumed oil, teach us that we are all sinners who have wandered from you and become lost in our own greed and egoism. Like the prodigal son who returns to his merciful father, lead us back to you and heal us from guilt. May the self-emptying love you gave on the cross be the transforming source of our forgiveness.

3. Ask one or more of the following questions:
   - What most intrigued you from this week's study?
   - Why is Luke's gospel often considered the good news of mercy and compassion?

4. Discuss lessons 19 through 24. Choose one or more of the questions for reflection and discussion from each lesson to talk over as a group.

5. Ask the group members to name one thing they have most appreciated about the way the group has worked during this Bible study. Ask group members to discuss any changes they might suggest in the way the group works in future studies.

6. Invite group members to complete lessons 25 through 30 on their own during the six days before the next meeting. They should write out their own answers to the questions as preparation for next week's session.

7. Discuss ways in which a better understanding of forgiveness could promote the healing of families and communities.

8. Conclude by praying aloud together the prayer at the end of one of the lessons discussed. You may want to conclude the prayer by asking members to voice prayers of thanksgiving.

This punishment by the majority is enough for such a person;
so now instead you should forgive and console him.

2 CORINTHIANS 2:6–7

Forgiveness and Reaffirming Love

2 CORINTHIANS 2:4–11 ⁴*For I wrote you out of much distress and anguish of heart and with many tears, not to cause you pain, but to let you know the abundant love that I have for you.*

⁵*But if anyone has caused pain, he has caused it not to me, but to some extent—not to exaggerate it—to all of you.* ⁶*This punishment by the majority is enough for such a person;* ⁷*so now instead you should forgive and console him, so that he may not be overwhelmed by excessive sorrow.* ⁸*So I urge you to reaffirm your love for him.* ⁹*I wrote for this reason: to test you and to know whether you are obedient in everything.* ¹⁰*Anyone whom you forgive, I also forgive. What I have forgiven, if I have forgiven anything, has been for your sake in the presence of Christ.* ¹¹*And we do this so that we may not be outwitted by Satan; for we are not ignorant of his designs.*

2 CORINTHIANS 5:14–19 ¹⁴*For the love of Christ urges us on, because we are convinced that one has died for all; therefore all have died.* ¹⁵*And he died for all, so that those who live might live no longer for themselves, but for him who died and was raised for them.*

¹⁶*From now on, therefore, we regard no one from a human point of view; even though we once knew Christ from a human point of view, we know him no longer*

in that way. [17]*So if anyone is in Christ, there is a new creation: everything old has passed away; see, everything has become new!* [18]*All this is from God, who reconciled us to himself through Christ, and has given us the ministry of reconciliation;* [19]*that is, in Christ God was reconciling the world to himself, not counting their trespasses against them, and entrusting the message of reconciliation to us.*

Paul's letter highlights the fact that neither sin nor forgiveness are private matters between individuals and God. Rather, the sins of one member of the community affect the whole church, so forgiveness also ought to be a communal concern. Paul writes about a sinner who has received a punishment for his sins by the consent of the community. He does not name the offender or tell us either his offense or the penalty imposed because the readers of his letter would have known all this. While Paul acknowledges that the pain caused by the sin has troubled everyone in the church, he states that now is the time to offer forgiveness (verses 5–8). The penalty inflicted by the church has apparently achieved its purpose in helping to bring about repentance. This accomplishment seems to be due not to the severity of the penalty but to the united conscience of the community challenging the offender. When repentance is sought in loving concern, rather than with a desire for retribution, both the community and the sinner mature in faith and integrity.

In urging the church to forgive the sinner, Paul offers two reasons for doing so. First, forgiveness will save the offender from falling too deeply into grief and self-condemnation (verse 7). Forgiveness creates the conditions for God's grace to work more profoundly within the sinner. Second, the community must forgive so that it will not be overcome by Satan (verse 11). For Paul, Satan is a conquered yet still dangerous foe who desires to divide the church and diminish its witness. The church that is unwilling to forgive will harm its power to evangelize and even destroy itself from within by its hypocrisy.

Paul's understanding of forgiveness is a result of the extraordinary sense of oneness he experiences with Christ, a unity that he knows is available to others through faith. His oneness with Christ is so profound that he uses the most intense language to describe it. He says that Christ has died for us all in such a way that we have all died to our old way of life. This reality requires a deep and abiding response on our part. Now we live no longer for ourselves but for Christ, "who died and was raised" for us (verses 14–15). His love for us, perfectly manifested in his death and resurrection, "urges us on," guiding our lives in the way of forgiveness.

Based on his own experience of conversion to Christ, Paul says that our ability to see Christ in a new way, not from "a human point of view" but from the standpoint of faith led by the Spirit, enables us to experience a transformed life (verse 16). In our dying and rising, we have become "a new creation," formed anew and participating in the remaking of the world which Christ has accomplished in his own dying and rising (verse 17). Victory over sin has been accomplished through him, and "in Christ" we share in that victory. We are brought from slavery in the realm of sin to the realm of life and freedom in Christ. Everything has become new!

The forgiveness and new life we have received impel us to share in the "ministry of reconciliation" (verses 18–19). For indeed, forgiveness is not just a private matter between individuals and God; it must be the communal mission of the church. Reconciled to God through Christ, we have been entrusted with "the message of reconciliation," the good news that we are at peace with God through Christ's cross and resurrection. And because we are reconciled with God, our reconciliation with one another should then follow.

Reflection and discussion

- How can it be said that there is no truly "private" sin, involving only the individual sinner and God?

- In what ways do our sins injure the church and put us in need of reconciliation with our brothers and sisters in Christ?

- How, according to Paul, does Satan seek to overcome the church? How does forgiveness defeat his designs?

- How can my words and actions become a more effective sign of Christ's forgiveness and contribute to the church's ministry of reconciliation?

Prayer

Lord Jesus Christ, who creates your people anew through your dying and rising, show me the victory that is mine as I live in you. Through faith and baptism, may I live more fully each day in the realm of freedom and forgiveness.

Be angry but do not sin; do not let the sun go down on your anger, and do not make room for the devil. EPHESIANS 4:26–27

Forgive As God in Christ Has Forgiven You

EPHESIANS 4:17–32 [17]*Now this I affirm and insist on in the Lord: you must no longer live as the Gentiles live, in the futility of their minds.* [18]*They are darkened in their understanding, alienated from the life of God because of their ignorance and hardness of heart.* [19]*They have lost all sensitivity and have abandoned themselves to licentiousness, greedy to practice every kind of impurity.* [20]*That is not the way you learned Christ!* [21]*For surely you have heard about him and were taught in him, as truth is in Jesus.* [22]*You were taught to put away your former way of life, your old self, corrupt and deluded by its lusts,* [23]*and to be renewed in the spirit of your minds,* [24]*and to clothe yourselves with the new self, created according to the likeness of God in true righteousness and holiness.*

[25]*So then, putting away falsehood, let all of us speak the truth to our neighbors, for we are members of one another.* [26]*Be angry but do not sin; do not let the sun go down on your anger,* [27]*and do not make room for the devil.* [28]*Thieves must give up stealing; rather let them labor and work honestly with their own hands, so as to have something to share with the needy.* [29]*Let no evil talk come out of your mouths, but only what is useful for building up, as there is need, so that your words may give grace to those who hear.* [30]*And do not grieve the Holy Spirit of God, with which you were marked with a seal for the day of redemption.* [31]*Put away from*

you all bitterness and wrath and anger and wrangling and slander, together with
all malice, [32]and be kind to one another, tender-hearted, forgiving one another, as
God in Christ has forgiven you.

Through the death and resurrection of Jesus Christ, the world has entered into a new era, and everyone has the opportunity to enter this renewal through conversion of heart, faith in Jesus, and Christian baptism. The Christian life, thus, consists not only in following the teachings of Jesus but also in embracing a new nature. Paul describes this radical transformation of life as the movement from the "old self" to the "new self."

Those living under the old, pagan way of life live in "futility," a life without meaning or value (verse 17). Deprived of the true source of light and the illumination that comes from God, they live in darkness (verse 18). Their "ignorance and hardness of heart" causes them to be alienated from God. Their separation of mind and heart from divine life leads to callousness and decadence, abandoning themselves to a wasteful life (verse 19). In contrast to this former way of life, Christians have learned a quite different way, the exact opposite of the pattern of life just described.

References to learning, hearing, and being taught refer to the process of hearing the gospel and the catechetical instruction involved in Christian initiation (verses 20–21). The contrast of light and darkness, the metaphor of clothing with the new self, and mention of the "seal" of the Holy Spirit (verse 30) indicate that the context is Christian baptism. The process of becoming a Christian, then, involves a renunciation of the old order and a transfer of allegiance to the new (verses 22–24). This new self, with its new way of life, indicates the close relationship between the intellectual awakening provided by Christian revelation and the moral transformation of life that it requires. What begins in baptism must be continued in a new way of living.

Paul's letter now spells out some of these new behavior patterns of a life lived in Christ. These begin with putting away falsehood and speaking the truth (verse 25). Without honesty, there can only be disunity. The list continues with an appeal to control anger lest it lead to sin (verse 26). Although there is nothing wrong with anger, and sometimes it can be a helpful emotion in response to injustice, the believer must not let anger seethe, because it can become the cause of sins like pride, hatred, or self-righteousness. The next exhortation seeks to end stealing, which is enriching oneself at the expense of someone else's labor (verse 28). Instead, honest manual labor allows a person not only to support oneself but also to share with those in need. In conversation, a Christian must not speak words of complaint, cynicism, and sarcasm, all of which demoralize others, but instead speak words that benefit those who listen (verse 29).

The presence of the Holy Spirit, whose seal is the Christian's mark of new allegiance and redemption in Christ, is reason enough to abolish bitterness, wrath, anger, wrangling, slander, and malice from one's speech (verses 30–31). In their place, the believer in Christ must manifest kindness and tender-heartedness, which promote a spirit of patience, tolerance, and acceptance (verse 32). Beyond that, those who live in Christ must continually forgive others on the strength of the example of forgiveness that Christ has given.

Reflection and discussion

- Is the effect of baptismal faith in my life so profound that it can be described as the movement from the "old self" to the "new self"?

- In what ways does my Christian faith give meaning and purpose to my life?

- Why is anger in itself not necessarily sinful? How can anger lead to sin that must be forgiven?

- From which of the offenses Paul names must I seek forgiveness from others?

- What behavioral changes might Paul counsel for my community?

Prayer

Lord Jesus Christ, through faith and baptism you make all things new for me. Give me the grace to continually forgive others as I have been forgiven in you. May I live in a way that manifests my new self in all that I say and do.

Bear with one another and, if anyone has a complaint against another, forgive each other; just as the Lord has forgiven you, so you also must forgive. COLOSSIANS 3:13

New Practices for a New Life

COLOSSIANS 3:1–17 ¹*So if you have been raised with Christ, seek the things that are above, where Christ is, seated at the right hand of God.* ²*Set your minds on things that are above, not on things that are on earth,* ³*for you have died, and your life is hidden with Christ in God.* ⁴*When Christ who is your life is revealed, then you also will be revealed with him in glory.*

⁵*Put to death, therefore, whatever in you is earthly: fornication, impurity, passion, evil desire, and greed (which is idolatry).* ⁶*On account of these the wrath of God is coming on those who are disobedient.* ⁷*These are the ways you also once followed, when you were living that life.*

⁸*But now you must get rid of all such things—anger, wrath, malice, slander, and abusive language from your mouth.* ⁹*Do not lie to one another, seeing that you have stripped off the old self with its practices* ¹⁰*and have clothed yourselves with the new self, which is being renewed in knowledge according to the image of its creator.* ¹¹*In that renewal there is no longer Greek and Jew, circumcised and uncircumcised, barbarian, Scythian, slave and free; but Christ is all and in all!*

¹²*As God's chosen ones, holy and beloved, clothe yourselves with compassion, kindness, humility, meekness, and patience.* ¹³*Bear with one another and, if anyone has a complaint against another, forgive each other; just as the Lord has forgiven you, so you also must forgive.* ¹⁴*Above all, clothe yourselves with love, which binds*

everything together in perfect harmony. ¹⁵*And let the peace of Christ rule in your* *hearts, to which indeed you were called in the one body. And be thankful.* ¹⁶*Let the* *word of Christ dwell in you richly; teach and admonish one another in all wisdom;* *and with gratitude in your hearts sing psalms, hymns, and spiritual songs to God.* ¹⁷*And whatever you do, in word or deed, do everything in the name of the Lord* *Jesus, giving thanks to God the Father through him.*

Through God's gift of faith and baptism, believers have been raised from death with Jesus Christ and share in that divine realm where he has been enthroned (verse 1). The language expresses a radical change of identity. This participation in Christ is not merely a future inheritance that Christians await; believers already share in his exaltation. Yet this new life is now "hidden with Christ in God"—that is, it cannot be fully seen or appreciated by the world (verse 3). This splendor of divine grace that fills our lives is even half-hidden from ourselves. But our lives in Christ will be fully revealed in the magnificent future for which we hope, when Christ is fully revealed in glory to all creation (verse 4).

For this reason, our identity in union with Christ is both a gift we have received and a call for which we are responsible. We are raised with Christ to be like him, but our identity with Christ is clearly not yet complete. Our baptismal rebirth requires that we become in practice what we truly are through the grace of the sacrament. This continuous process means dying to all within us that is selfish, debased, and sinful (verses 5–9), and rising to a life that reflects "the image of its creator" (verse 10). Although man and woman were created in God's image, they distorted that image through sin. But, through Christ, God is at work restoring that divine image in humanity.

Because the risen Christ lives in his followers, racial, religious, cultural, and social barriers no longer divide them (verse 11). Paul uses baptismal language in describing this transformation: stripping off "the old self" and clothing with "the new self." This new life—as God's chosen, holy, and beloved ones—is characterized by "compassion, kindness, humility, meekness, and patience" (verse 12). Notably, these virtues are used to describe God and Christ in other parts of Paul's writings. Therefore, because we have been united to Christ in faith and baptism, we are to put on these divine qualities in our relationships toward others. As we strip off those vices associated with the old self, we clothe ourselves with virtues that have the well-being of others as their primary goal.

This process of becoming in daily life who we truly are in Christ requires a great deal of forbearance and forgiveness of one another (verse 13). God's grace does not automatically transform a sinful, earthly person into a new creation who practices virtues characteristic of God. But God's gift of forgiveness, which we have all received, becomes the means of helping one another with the continual challenges of transformation in Christ. This forgiveness in not just a tool for easing over misunderstandings; rather, it is the essential means of conforming ourselves to the image of God in Christian community. "Just as the Lord has forgiven you," Paul exhorts, "so you also must forgive." This is a clear reference to the teaching of Jesus, especially as it is expressed in the Lord's Prayer. This daily prayer of the church may have already served for the Colossians as a regular reminder of the need for forgiveness in the everyday life of the Christian community.

The community at Colossae read aloud Paul's letter in the church's liturgy. He commends them to put on love, the final garment to be put on over all the clothing of the new self (verse 14). He urges his hearers to let Christ's peace reign in their hearts and to be thankful (verse 15). And then he refers to "the word of Christ," wise teaching, and songs of worship—all hints that Paul's letter is read in the liturgical assembly (verse 16). When we allow "the word of Christ" to dwell with us through the sacred Scriptures, Christian teaching to mature our minds, and songs of praise to fill our souls, then our communal worship of God will expand into our daily living, so that we will "do everything in the name of the Lord Jesus" and our lives will become a thanksgiving sacrifice offered to God the Father (verse 17).

Reflection and discussion

- What is the relationship between the sacraments of baptism and Eucharist and my daily life in Christ?

- In what ways is my new life still "hidden"? In what ways has it been "revealed" to the world?

- What encouragement in this passage is most helpful or motivating to me?

Prayer

Lord Jesus Christ, raised and seated at the right hand of God, renew my mind and heart so that my first desire is to imitate you. Forgive me for my failings, and give me the grace to forgive others.

"I will remember their sins and their lawless deeds no more."
Where there is forgiveness of these, there is no longer
any offering for sin. HEBREWS 10:17–18

One Offering for the Forgiveness of Sin

HEBREWS 10:1–18 ¹*Since the law has only a shadow of the good things to come and not the true form of these realities, it can never, by the same sacrifices that are continually offered year after year, make perfect those who approach.* ²*Otherwise, would they not have ceased being offered, since the worshipers, cleansed once for all, would no longer have any consciousness of sin?* ³*But in these sacrifices there is a reminder of sin year after year.* ⁴*For it is impossible for the blood of bulls and goats to take away sins.* ⁵*Consequently, when Christ came into the world, he said,*

> *"Sacrifices and offerings you have not desired,*
> > *but a body you have prepared for me;*
> ⁶*in burnt offerings and sin offerings*
> > *you have taken no pleasure.*
> ⁷*Then I said, 'See, God, I have come to do your will, O God'*
> > *(in the scroll of the book it is written of me)."*

⁸*When he said above, "You have neither desired nor taken pleasure in sacrifices and offerings and burnt offerings and sin offerings" (these are offered according to the law),* ⁹*then he added, "See, I have come to do your will." He abolishes the first in order to establish the second.* ¹⁰*And it is by God's will that we have been sanctified through the offering of the body of Jesus Christ once for all.*

¹¹*And every priest stands day after day at his service, offering again and again the same sacrifices that can never take away sins.* ¹²*But when Christ had offered for all time a single sacrifice for sins, "he sat down at the right hand of God,"* ¹³*and since then has been waiting "until his enemies would be made a footstool for his feet."* ¹⁴*For by a single offering he has perfected for all time those who are sanctified.* ¹⁵*And the Holy Spirit also testifies to us, for after saying,*

¹⁶*"This is the covenant that I will make with them*
after those days, says the Lord:
I will put my laws in their hearts,
and I will write them on their minds,"
¹⁷*he also adds,*
"I will remember their sins and their lawless deeds no more."
¹⁸*Where there is forgiveness of these, there is no longer any offering for sin.*

The sacrifices of the old covenant were a "shadow" of the sacrifice of Jesus Christ (verse 1). But now, in him, "the true form of these realities" has been revealed to us. These sacrifices prescribed in the Torah of Moses brought a ritual and temporary cleansing of sin, but they were never able to bring about the kind of forgiveness that would bring people inner peace. They were unable to inwardly heal the human conscience from guilt. In fact, these sacrifices were repeated reminders of sin that continually emphasized human guilt and unworthiness before God (verses 2–4). The ancient sacrifices were incomplete and repetitious, whereas the once-for-all sacrifice of Christ is perfectly complete. In fact, Christ's sacrifice not only cleanses us but makes us holy and able to come into the very presence of God.

The new covenant offers us a way to receive authentic forgiveness of sins. The author of Hebrews places the words of Psalm 40 on the lips of Jesus (verses 5–9). The obedient will of Jesus, who offered his body and shed his blood, fulfills and completes the numerous sacrifices of old. Because of who Christ is and the nature of his self-offering, he offers us complete and interior forgiveness, absolving our consciences of guilt. In Christ, we need not try to make up for our sins by our own deeds, even if that were possible. Instead, Christ has taken up all our sins and guilt as well as their death-dealing consequences, and offers us true and lasting forgiveness.

The author holds up two images for our reflection. The first is of the many priests standing in the temple, offering sacrifices each day, repetitively trying to bring about forgiveness of sins for those who come to worship (verse 11). The second is of one priest, who made one perfect offering for sins, and is now seated at the place of authority with God (verse 12). The priests of the temple are standing, a sign of repeated action that can never be completed, but Christ is seated, having accomplished his all-sufficient work. Having won the victory, Christ is now waiting for the results (verse 13). He waits for all his enemies to be made his footstool: injustice, hatred, despair, loneliness, sickness, and death. Between Christ's sacrifice on the cross and his return in glory, we are being perfected and sanctified (verse 14).

The sacrifice of the new covenant is "the offering of the body of Jesus Christ once for all" (verse 10). Yet, through the church's eucharistic assembly, the one, eternal sacrifice is made present on altars throughout the world until he comes again. The memorial of his ageless sacrifice transcends space and time, making us participants in his own offering at the throne of the Father. Christ is always making intercession for us, removing the barrier between sinners and our forgiving God. The body and blood of Jesus, offered for us in sacrifice and received in Communion, invites us to truly experience God's merciful forgiveness while our sanctification is being perfected.

Reflection and discussion

- What was the function of the ancient law of animal sacrifice? In what sense did those many sacrifices of the old covenant foreshadow the sacrifice of Christ?

- In what sense do I believe the sacrifice of Christ is now complete? In what sense do I await the complete effects of his once-for-all sacrifice?

- How can the one, eternal sacrifice of Christ offer me complete and lasting forgiveness?

- Do I allow myself to experience the complete forgiveness that God wants to give me through the sacrifice of Christ's body and blood?

Prayer

Eternal High Priest, who offered your body as a perfect offering for sin, give me the grace to experience your complete forgiveness. Make me holy so that I may draw near to you and share deeply in your divine life.

Confess your sins to one another, and pray for one another, so that you may be healed. The prayer of the righteous is powerful and effective. JAMES 5:16

Confess Your Sins to One Another

JAMES 5:13–20 [13]*Are any among you suffering? They should pray. Are any cheerful? They should sing songs of praise.* [14]*Are any among you sick? They should call for the elders of the church and have them pray over them, anointing them with oil in the name of the Lord.* [15]*The prayer of faith will save the sick, and the Lord will raise them up; and anyone who has committed sins will be forgiven.* [16]*Therefore confess your sins to one another, and pray for one another, so that you may be healed. The prayer of the righteous is powerful and effective.* [17]*Elijah was a human being like us, and he prayed fervently that it might not rain, and for three years and six months it did not rain on the earth.* [18]*Then he prayed again, and the heaven gave rain and the earth yielded its harvest.*

[19]*My brothers and sisters, if anyone among you wanders from the truth and is brought back by another,* [20]*you should know that whoever brings back a sinner from wandering will save the sinner's soul from death and will cover a multitude of sins.*

James offers readers a glimpse into the communal life of the early church, a community composed of suffering, praying, cheerful, singing, sick, sinning, and faith-filled people (verses 13–14). He particularly spotlights the importance of prayer for the healing of the sick and the sinful (verse 15). The counsel to "call for the elders" suggests that the anointing with oil and prayer for healing has already become a formal ministry in the church. James confidently assures his hearers of the saving power of this "prayer of faith." The sick persons will be raised up and their sins will be forgiven.

The close relationship of sickness and sin is characteristic of the ancient world. In his own ministry, Jesus first forgave the paralytic of his sins and then restored him to full health. The physical healing removed any doubt that the paralytic was restored in his relationship to God. This link between sin and sickness is not to suggest necessarily that one is the cause of the other; in fact, Jesus himself rejects this common belief. But today's holistic understanding of healing confirms the ancient instinct that forgiveness and freedom from guilt is essential to physical, mental, emotional, and spiritual health. This abiding relationship in the early church between confession, forgiveness, healing, and health must not be forgotten. Jesus' ministry continues through the ages in his church, as the Spirit-led community prays and acts "in the name of the Lord."

James urges the community to do two things for their healing: first, "confess your sins to one another," and second, "pray for one another" (verse 16). This suggests a communal ritual of confession, repentance, forgiveness, and healing. Confession of sins aloud and to another person strengthens truthfulness and undermines pride, which is the root of all sin. James assures each person of the power of prayer by citing the example of Elijah. Although he was "a human being like us," James says, "he prayed fervently," shutting and opening the heavens (verses 17–18). If a human being can pray so fervently that God provides drought and rain, then surely we can pray with enough faith to receive forgiveness and healing.

James concludes his letter with an emphasis on the responsibility of members of the church for one another (verses 19–20). Christians must exhort and admonish one another, seeking out those who err and go astray. The stakes are high. One who rescues a sinner, bringing back another to the way of salvation, saves the sinner's soul from spiritual death. The response of Christians to sinners must not be judgment but restoration, reaching out and helping the person reverse course and get back on the path. The rescue results in the forgiveness of "a multitude of sins," covered over by God's grace and forgotten forever. The rescued one then rejoins the church, the community in which all are forgiven sinners.

Reflection and discussion

- In what ways does confessing the sins of resentment, holding grudges, and unforgiven injuries lead to physical, mental, emotional, and spiritual healing?

- What might be some of the positive effects of performing the church's healing ministry in the context of communal prayer?

- What more could I do to draw on the forgiving and healing power that Jesus has given to his church?

Prayer

Merciful Savior, you care for us in our sin and our illness, and you call us to care for one another. Help us trust in you, whose power offers us forgiveness and healing in this life and salvation in eternal life.

If we confess our sins, he who is faithful and just will forgive us our sins and cleanse us from all unrighteousness.

1 JOHN 1:9

Admitting Our Sins and Seeking the Truth

1 JOHN 1:5–10 *⁵This is the message we have heard from him and proclaim to you, that God is light and in him there is no darkness at all. ⁶If we say that we have fellowship with him while we are walking in darkness, we lie and do not do what is true; ⁷but if we walk in the light as he himself is in the light, we have fellowship with one another, and the blood of Jesus his Son cleanses us from all sin. ⁸If we say that we have no sin, we deceive ourselves, and the truth is not in us. ⁹If we confess our sins, he who is faithful and just will forgive us our sins and cleanse us from all unrighteousness. ¹⁰If we say that we have not sinned, we make him a liar, and his word is not in us.*

"God is light" (verse 5). This is the message that John proclaims in his letter, a message that God has given the world. Light describes God's essential nature and also God's relationship to humanity. It implies truthfulness, authenticity, and holiness. Light's most essential characteristic is to shine, to manifest itself, to reveal, and this God has done most completely in Christ, who is the light of the world. God is not only light in the abstract, but through Jesus this divine light has been shown in such a way as to truly illumine human life.

In contrast, darkness is the absence of light, the absence of God. It implies deceit, evil, and sin. While in God "there is no darkness," in human character and behavior there is always light and shadow, gray and shade. The reality of God shining into the world in Christ forms the basis not only of Christian proclamation and belief but also of Christian response in action. "If we walk in the light," then we live in God's sphere of being; we live an authentic life in fellowship with God, a life in the truth (verses 6–7). The standard for this way of life is Jesus Christ, the way, the truth, and the life.

Walking in the light results in two consequences: first, "we have fellowship with one another," united in community with other disciples of Jesus; and second, the blood of Jesus "cleanses us from all sin." The closer our fellowship with God and other Christians, the more aware we will be of sin in our own life. Denying our sinfulness is self-deception (verse 8). But by confessing our sins, God forgives us and cleanses our lives from evil (verse 9).

Acknowledging our own sinfulness and our need to be forgiven is the essential starting point for walking in the light. If we don't see sin in our lives or the need for God's forgiveness, we make ourselves blind. We walk in the darkness of our own inability or refusal to see the reality of our humanity. We may deflect our sinfulness by telling ourselves that we have good intentions or by claiming that we're not as bad as other people. Or we avoid our sin by attempting to be so compulsively perfect that we deny that we have any problems. Or we may exaggerate our guilt in order to convince others that we are so ashamed that we deserve forgiveness. But self-deceit, deflection, avoidance, denial, and exaggeration do not lead to real conversion of life. Only truth and honesty—with God, others, and ourselves—bring about change and growth (verses 8, 10). If we claim we have not sinned, then we make God a liar, we deceive ourselves, and our lives are a sham.

We have been cleansed from sin through the sacrificial blood of Jesus on the cross. Through baptism, confession, repentance, absolution, prayer, and Eucharist, we receive forgiveness for our sins and move from the darkness into the light. Only by walking in the light do we open our lives to be transformed by God's grace and live a genuinely human life.

Reflection and discussion

- What are some of the reasons I might lie to myself, to others, or to God about my need for forgiveness?

- According to the text, why do I need forgiveness?

- How will I open my life today to God's forgiveness and transforming grace?

Prayer

Light of the world, who calls us to live in honesty and truth, help me to recognize those areas of my life in which I stand in need of your healing forgiveness. Help me see my life rightly, confess my sins, and walk in your light.

SUGGESTIONS FOR FACILITATORS, GROUP SESSION 6

1. Welcome group members and make any final announcements or requests.

2. You may want to pray this prayer as a group:
   Savior of the world, who has made all things new through your life, death, and resurrection, fill us with your grace so that we may draw near to you and share deeply in your divine life. Through the transforming power of these sacred Scriptures, give us the desire to recognize those areas of our lives that need your healing, to admit our failings, to forgive others as we have been forgiven in you, and to live in freedom more fully each day. Help us to trust in you and to live always in your light.

3. Ask one or more of the following questions:
   - How has this study of forgiveness deepened your life in Christ?
   - In what way has this study challenged you the most?

4. Discuss lessons 25 through 30. Choose one or more of the questions for reflection and discussion from each lesson to discuss as a group.

5. Ask the group if they would like to study another in the *Threshold Bible Study* series. Discuss the topic and dates, and make a decision among those interested. Ask the group members to suggest people they would like to invite to participate in the next study series.

6. Ask the group to discuss the insights that stand out most from this study over the past six weeks.

7. Conclude by praying aloud the following prayer or another of your own choosing:
   Holy Spirit of the living God, you inspired the writers of the Scriptures and you have guided our study during these weeks. Continue to deepen our love for the word of God in the holy Scriptures, and draw us more deeply into the heart of Jesus. Thank you for your merciful, gracious, steadfast, and faithful love.